AF680650

Health and Safety at Work etc. Act 1974

CHAPTER 37

Explanatory Notes are available separately

GRAN*GIS* UK Publishing

Adapted and published by GRANGIS (Grand Register Library).
Online: www.grangis.com
E-mail: contact@grangis.com

In this version:
ISBN: 979-8-88559-097-6

Note: This is the original version (as it was originally enacted). Title, sub-title and the generated date is as marked on the pages.

Health and Safety at Work etc. Act 1974

CHAPTER 37

HEALTH AND SAFETY AT WORK ETC. ACT 1974

PART I

HEALTH, SAFETY AND WELFARE IN CONNECTION WITH WORK, AND CONTROL OF DANGEROUS SUBSTANCES AND CERTAIN EMISSIONS INTO THE ATMOSPHERE

Preliminary

General duties

The Health and Safety Commission and the Health and Safety Executive

PART IV

MISCELLANEOUS AND GENERAL

SCHEDULES

Health and Safety at Work etc. Act 1974

1974 CHAPTER 37

An Act to make further provision for securing the health, safety and welfare of persons at work, for protecting others against risks to health or safety in connection with the activities of persons at work, for controlling the keeping and use and preventing the unlawful acquisition, possession and use of dangerous substances, and for controlling certain emissions into the atmosphere; to make further provision with respect to the employment medical advisory service; to amend the law relating to building regulations, and the Building (Scotland) Act 1959; and for connected purposes. [31st July 1974]

BE IT ENACTED by the Queen's most Excellent Majesty, by and with the advice and consent of the Lords Spiritual and Temporal, and Commons, in this present Parliament assembled, and by the authority of the same, as follows:—

PART I

HEALTH, SAFETY AND WELFARE IN CONNECTION WITH WORK, AND CONTROL OF DANGEROUS SUBSTANCES AND CERTAIN EMISSIONS INTO THE ATMOSPHERE

Preliminary

1 Preliminary

(1) The provisions of this Part shall have effect with a view to—

(a) securing the health, safety and welfare of persons at work;

(b) protecting persons other than persons at work against risks to health or safety arising out of or in connection with the activities of persons at work;

(c) controlling the keeping and use of explosive or highly flammable or otherwise dangerous substances, and generally preventing the unlawful acquisition, possession and use of such substances ; and

(d) controlling the emission into the atmosphere of noxious or offensive substances from premises of any class prescribed for the purposes of this paragraph.

(2) The provisions of this Part relating to the making of health and safety regulations and agricultural health and safety regulations and the preparation and approval of codes of practice shall in particular have effect with a view to enabling the enactments specified in the third column of Schedule 1 and the regulations, orders and other instruments in force under those enactments to be progressively replaced by a system of regulations and approved codes of practice operating in combination with the other provisions of this Part and designed to maintain or improve the standards of health, safety and welfare established by or under those enactments.

(3) For the purposes of this Part risks arising out of or in connection with the activities of persons at work shall be treated as including risks attributable to the manner of conducting an undertaking, the plant or substances used for the purposes of an undertaking and the condition of premises so used or any part of them.

(4) References in this Part to the general purposes of this Part are references to the purposes mentioned in subsection (1) above.

General duties

2 General duties of employers to their employees

(1) It shall be the duty of every employer to ensure, so far as is reasonably practicable, the health, safety and welfare at work of all his employees.

(2) Without prejudice to the generality of an employer's duty under the preceding subsection, the matters to which that duty extends include in particular—

(a) the provision and maintenance of plant and systems of work that are, so far as is reasonably practicable, safe and without risks to health ;

(b) arrangements for ensuring, so far as is reasonably practicable, safety and absence of risks to health in connection with the use, handling, storage and transport of articles and substances ;

(c) the provision of such information, instruction, training and supervision as is necessary to ensure, so far as is reasonably practicable, the health and safety at work of his employees;

(d) so far as is reasonably practicable as regards any place of work under the employer's control, the maintenance of it in a condition that is safe and without risks to health and the provision and maintenance of means of access to and egress from it that are safe and without such risks;

(e) the provision and maintenance of a working environment for his employees that is, so far as is reasonably practicable, safe, without risks to health, and adequate as regards facilities and arrangements for their welfare at work.

(3) Except in such cases as may be prescribed, it shall be the duty of every employer to prepare and as often as may be appropriate revise a written statement of his general policy with respect to the health and safety at work of his employees and the organisation and arrangements for the time being in force for carrying out that policy, and to bring the statement and any revision of it to the notice of all of his employees.

(4) Regulations made by the Secretary of State may provide for the appointment in prescribed cases by recognised trade unions (within the meaning of the regulations) of safety representatives from amongst the employees, and those representatives shall represent the employees in consultations with the employers under subsection (6) below and shall have such other functions as may be prescribed.

(5) Regulations made by the Secretary of State may provide for the election in prescribed cases by employees of safety representatives from amongst the employees, and those representatives shall represent the employees in consultations with the employers under subsection (6) below and may have such other functions as may be prescribed.

(6) It shall be the duty of every employer to consult any such representatives with a view to the making and maintenance of arrangements which will enable him and his employees to cooperate effectively in promoting and developing measures to ensure the health and safety at work of the employees, and in checking the effectiveness of such measures.

(7) In such cases as may be prescribed it shall be the duty of every employer, if requested to do so by the safety representatives mentioned in subsections (4) and (5) above, to establish, in accordance with regulations made by the Secretary of State, a safety committee having the function of keeping under review the measures taken to ensure the health and safety at work of his employees and such other functions as may be prescribed.

3 General duties of employers and self-employed to persons other than their employees

(1) It shall be the duty of every employer to conduct his undertaking in such a way as to ensure, so far as is reasonably practicable, that persons not in his employment who may be affected thereby are not thereby exposed to risks to their health or safety.

(2) It shall be the duty of every self-employed person to conduct his undertaking in such a way as to ensure, so far as is reasonably practicable, that he and other persons (not being his employees) who may be affected thereby are not thereby exposed to risks to their health or safety.

(3) In such cases as may be prescribed, it shall be the duty of every employer and every self-employed person, in the prescribed circumstances and in the prescribed manner, to give to persons (not being his employees) who may be affected by the way in which he conducts his undertaking the prescribed information about such aspects of the way in which he conducts his undertaking as might affect their health or safety.

4 General duties of persons concerned with premises to persons other than their employees

(1) This section has effect for imposing on persons duties in relation to those who—
- (a) are not their employees ; but
- (b) use non-domestic premises made available to them as a place of work or as a place where they may use plant or substances provided for their use there,

and applies to premises so made available and other non-domestic premises used in connection with them.

(2) It shall be the duty of each person who has, to any extent, control of premises to which this section applies or of the means of access thereto or egress therefrom or of any plant or substance in such premises to take such measures as it is reasonable for a person in his position to take to ensure, so far as is reasonably practicable, that the premises, all means of access thereto or egress therefrom available for use by persons using the premises, and any plant or substance in the premises or, as the case may be, provided for use there, is or are safe and without risks to health.

(3) Where a person has, by virtue of any contract or tenancy, an obligation of any extent in relation to—

(a) the maintenance or repair of any premises to which this section applies or any means of access thereto or egress therefrom; or

(b) the safety of or the absence of risks to health arising from plant or substances in any such premises ;

that person shall be treated, for the purposes of subsection (2) above, as being a person who has control of the matters to which his obligation extends.

(4) Any reference in this section to a person having control of any premises or matter is a reference to a person having control of the premises or matter in connection with the carrying on by him of a trade, business or other undertaking (whether for profit or not).

5 General duty of persons in control of certain premises in relation to harmful emissions into atmosphere

(1) It shall be the duty of the person having control of any premises of a class prescribed for the purposes of section 1(1)(d) to use the best practicable means for preventing the emission into the atmosphere from the premises of noxious or offensive substances and for rendering harmless and inoffensive such substances as may be so emitted.

(2) The reference in subsection (1) above to the means to be used for the purposes there mentioned includes a reference to the manner in which the plant provided for those purposes is used and to the supervision of any operation involving the emission of the substances to which that subsection applies.

(3) Any substance or a substance of any description prescribed for the purposes of subsection (1) above as noxious or offensive shall be a noxious or, as the case may be, an offensive substance for those purposes whether or not it would be so apart from this subsection.

(4) Any reference in this section to a person having control of any premises is a reference to a person having control of the premises in connection with the carrying on by him of a trade, business or other undertaking (whether for profit or not) and any duty imposed on any such person by this section shall extend only to matters within his control.

6 General duties of manufacturers etc. as regards articles and substances for use at work

(1) It shall be the duty of any person who designs, manufactures, imports or supplies any article for use at work—

(a) to ensure, so far as is reasonably practicable, that the article is so designed and constructed as to be safe and without risks to health when properly used ;

(b) to carry out or arrange for the carrying out of such testing and examination as may be necessary for the performance of the duty imposed on him by the preceding paragraph;

(c) to take such steps as are necessary to secure that there will be available in connection with the use of the article at work adequate information about the use for which it is designed and has been tested, and about any conditions necessary to ensure that, when put to that use, it will be safe and without risks to health.

(2) It shall be the duty of any person who undertakes the design or manufacture of any article for use at work to carry out or arrange for the carrying out of any necessary research with a view to the discovery and, so far as is reasonably practicable, the elimination or minimisation of any risks to health or safety to which the design or article may give rise.

(3) It shall be the duty of any person who erects or installs any article for use at work in any premises where that article is to be used by persons at work to ensure, so far as is reasonably practicable, that nothing about the way in which it is erected or installed makes it unsafe or a risk to health when properly used.

(4) It shall be the duty of any person who manufactures, imports or supplies any substance for use at work—

(a) to ensure, so far as is reasonably practicable, that the substance is safe and without risks to health when properly used;

(b) to carry out or arrange for the carrying out of such testing and examination as may be necessary for the performance of the duty imposed on him by the preceding paragraph;

(c) to take such steps as are necessary to secure that there will be available in connection with the use of the substance at work adequate information about the results of any relevant tests which have been carried out on or in connection with the substance and about any conditions necessary to ensure that it will be safe and without risks to health when properly used.

(5) It shall be the duty of any person who undertakes the manufacture of any substance for use at work to carry out or arrange for the carrying out of any necessary research with a view to the discovery and, so far as is reasonably practicable, the elimination or minimisation of any risks to health or safety to which the substance may give rise.

(6) Nothing in the preceding provisions of this section shall be taken to require a person to repeat any testing, examination or research which has been carried out otherwise than by him or at his instance, in so far as it is reasonable for him to rely on the results thereof for the purposes of those provisions.

(7) Any duty imposed on any person by any of the preceding provisions of this section shall extend only to things done in the course of a trade, business or other undertaking carried on by him (whether for profit or not) and to matters within his control.

(8) Where a person designs, manufactures, imports or supplies an article for or to another on the basis of a written undertaking by that other to take specified steps sufficient to ensure, so far as is reasonably practicable, that the article will be safe and without risks to health when properly used, the undertaking shall have the effect of relieving the first-mentioned person from the duty imposed by subsection (1)(a) above to such extent as is reasonable having regard to the terms of the undertaking.

(9) Where a person (" the ostensible supplier ") supplies any article for use at work or substance for use at work to another (" the customer ") under a hire-purchase agreement, conditional sale agreement or credit-sale agreement, and the ostensible supplier—

(a) carries on the business of financing the acquisition of goods by others by means of such agreements; and

(b) in the course of that business acquired his interest in the article or substance supplied to the customer as a means of financing its acquisition by the customer from a third person (" the effective supplier "),

the effective supplier and not the ostensible supplier shall be treated for the purposes of this section as supplying the article or substance to the customer, and any duty imposed by the preceding provisions of this section on suppliers shall accordingly fall on the effective supplier and not on the ostensible supplier.

(10) For the purposes of this section an article or substance is not to be regarded as properly used where it is used without regard to any relevant information or advice relating to its use which has been made available by a person by whom it was designed, manufactured, imported or supplied.

7 General duties of employees at work

It shall be the duty of every employee while at work—

(a) to take reasonable care for the health and safety of himself and of other persons who may be affected by his acts or omissions at work; and

(b) as regards any duty or requirement imposed on his employer or any other person by or under any of the relevant statutory provisions, to co-operate with him so far as is necessary to enable that duty or requirement to be performed or complied with.

8 Duty not to interfere with or misuse things provided pursuant to certain provisions

No person shall intentionally or recklessly interfere with or misuse anything provided in the interests of health, safety or welfare in pursuance of any of the relevant statutory provisions.

9 Duty not to charge employees for things done or provided pursuant to certain specific requirements

No employer shall levy or permit to be levied on any employee of his any charge in respect of anything done or provided in pursuance of any specific requirement of the relevant statutory provisions.

The Health and Safety Commission and the Health and Safety Executive

10 Establishment of the Commission and the Executive

(1) There shall be two bodies corporate to be called the Health and Safety Commission and the Health and Safety Executive which shall be constituted in accordance with the following provisions of this section.

(2) The Health and Safety Commission (hereafter in this Act referred to as " the Commission ") shall consist of a chairman appointed by the Secretary of State and not less than six nor more than nine other members appointed by the Secretary of State in accordance with subsection (3) below.

(3) Before appointing the members of the Commission (other than the chairman) the Secretary of State shall—

(a) as to three of them, consult such organisations representing employers as he considers appropriate ;

(b) as to three others, consult such organisations representing employees as he considers appropriate; and

(c) as to any other members he may appoint, consult such organisations representing local authorities and such other organisations, including professional bodies, the activities of whose members are concerned with matters relating to any of the general purposes of this Part, as he considers appropriate.

(4) The Secretary of State may appoint one of the members to be deputy chairman of the Commission.

(5) The Health and Safety Executive (hereafter in this Act referred to as " the Executive ") shall consist of three persons of whom one shall be appointed by the Commission with the approval of the Secretary of State to be the director of the Executive and the others shall be appointed by the Commission with the like approval after consultation with the said director.

(6) The provisions of Schedule 2 shall have effect with respect to the Commission and the Executive.

(7) The functions of the Commission and of the Executive, and of their officers and servants, shall be performed on behalf of the Crown.

11 General functions of the Commission and the Executive

(1) In addition to the other functions conferred on the Commission by virtue of this Act, but subject to subsection (3) below, it shall be the general duty of the Commission to do such things and make such arrangements as it considers appropriate for the general purposes of this Part except as regards matters relating exclusively to agricultural operations.

(2) It shall be the duty of the Commission, except as aforesaid—

(a) to assist and encourage persons concerned with matters relevant to any of the general purposes of this Part to further those purposes;

(b) to make such arrangements as it considers appropriate for the carrying out of research, the publication of the results of research and the provision of training and information in connection with those purposes, and to encourage research and the provision of training and information in that connection by others ;

(c) to make such arrangements as it considers appropriate for securing that government departments, employers, employees, organisations representing employers and employees respectively, and other persons concerned with matters relevant to any of those purposes are provided with an information and advisory service and are kept informed of, and adequately advised on, such matters;

(d) to submit from time to time to the authority having power to make regulations under any of the relevant statutory provisions such proposals as the Commission considers appropriate for the making of regulations under that power.

(3) It shall be the duty of the Commission—

(a) to submit to the Secretary of State from time to time particulars of what it proposes to do for the purpose of performing its functions ; and

(b) subject to the following paragraph, to ensure that its activities are in accordance with proposals approved by the Secretary of State; and

(c) to give effect to any directions given to it by the Secretary of State.

(4) In addition to any other functions conferred on the Executive by virtue of this Part, it shall be the duty of the Executive—

(a) to exercise on behalf of the Commission such of the Commission's functions as the Commission directs it to exercise; and

(b) to give effect to any directions given to it by the Commission otherwise than in pursuance of paragraph (a) above;

but, except for the purpose of giving effect to directions given to the Commission by the Secretary of State, the Commission shall not give to the Executive any directions as to the enforcement of any of the relevant statutory provisions in a particular case.

(5) Without prejudice to subsection (2) above, it shall be the duty of the Executive, if so requested by a Minister of the Crown—

(a) to provide him with information about the activities of the Executive in connection with any matter with which he is concerned ; and

(b) to provide him with advice on any matter with which he is concerned on which relevant expert advice is obtainable from any of the officers or servants of the Executive but which is not relevant to any of the general purposes of this Part.

(6) The Commission and the Executive shall, subject to any directions given to it in pursuance of this Part, have power to do anything (except borrow money) which is calculated to facilitate, or is conducive or incidental to, the performance of any function of the Commission or, as the case may be, the Executive (including a function conferred on it by virtue of this subsection).

12 Control of the Commission by the Secretary of State

The Secretary of State may—

(a) approve, with or without modifications, any proposals submitted to him in pursuance of section 11 (3)(a);

(b) give to the Commission at any time such directions as he thinks fit with respect to its functions (including directions modifying its functions, but not directions conferring on it functions other than any of which it was deprived by previous directions given by virtue of this paragraph), and any directions which it appears to him requisite or expedient to give in the interests of the safety of the State.

13 Other powers of the Commission

(1) The Commission shall have power—

(a) to make agreements with any government department or other person for that department or person to perform on behalf of the Commission or the Executive (with or without payment) any of the functions of the Commission or, as the case may be, of the Executive;

(b) subject to subsection (2) below, to make agreements with any Minister of the Crown, government department or other public authority for the Commission to perform on behalf of that Minister, department or authority (with or without payment) functions exercisable by the Minister, department or authority (including, in the case of a Minister, functions not conferred by an enactment), being functions which in the opinion of the Secretary of State can appropriately be performed by the Commission in connection with any of the Commission's functions;

(c) to provide (with or without payment) services or facilities required otherwise than for the general purposes of this Part in so far as they are required by any government department or other public authority in connection with the exercise by that department or authority of any of its functions;

(d) to appoint persons or committees of persons to provide the Commission with advice in connection with any of its functions and (without prejudice to the generality of the following paragraph) to pay to persons so appointed such remuneration as the Secretary of State may with the approval of the Minister for the Civil Service determine;

(e) in connection with any of the functions of the Commission, to pay to any person such travelling and subsistence allowances and such compensation for loss of remunerative time as the Secretary of State may with the approval of the Minister for the Civil Service determine;

(f) to carry out or arrange for or make payments in respect of research into any matter connected with any of the Commission's functions, and to disseminate or arrange for or make payments in respect of the dissemination of information derived from such research ;

(g) to include, in any arrangements made by the Commission for the provision of facilities or services by it or on its behalf, provision for the making of payments to the Commission or any person acting on its behalf by other parties to the arrangements and by persons who use those facilities or services.

(2) Nothing in subsection (1)(b) shall authorise the Commission to perform any function of a Minister, department or authority which consists of a power to make regulations or other instruments of a legislative character.

14 Power of the Commission to direct investigations and inquiries

(1) This section applies to the following matters, that is to say any accident, occurrence, situation or other matter whatsoever which the Commission thinks it necessary or expedient to investigate for any of the general purposes of this Part or with a view to the making of regulations for those purposes; and for the purposes of this subsection it is immaterial whether the Executive is or is not responsible for securing the enforcement of such (if any) of the relevant statutory provisions as relate to the matter in question.

(2) The Commission may at any time—

(a) direct the Executive or authorise any other person to investigate and make a special report on any matter to which this section applies ; or

(b) with the consent of the Secretary of State direct an inquiry to be held into any such matter;

but shall not do so in any particular case that appears to the Commission to involve only matters relating exclusively to agricultural operations.

(3) Any inquiry held by virtue of subsection (2)(b) above shall be held in accordance with regulations made for the purposes of this subsection by the Secretary of State, and shall be held in public except where or to the extent that the regulations provide otherwise.

(4) Regulations made for the purposes of subsection (3) above may in particular include provision—

(a) conferring on the person holding any such inquiry, and any person assisting him in the inquiry, powers of entry and inspection;

(b) conferring on any such person powers of summoning witnesses to give evidence or produce documents and power to take evidence on oath and administer oaths or require the making of declarations ;

(c) requiring any such inquiry to be held otherwise than in public where or to the extent that a Minister of the Crown so directs.

(5) In the case of a special report made by virtue of subsection (2)(a) above or a report made by the person holding an inquiry held by virtue of subsection (2)(b) above, the Commission may cause the report, or so much of it as the Commission thinks fit, to be made public at such time and in such manner as the Commission thinks fit.

(6) The Commission—

(a) in the case of an investigation and special report made by virtue of subsection (2)(a) above (otherwise than by an officer or servant of the Executive), may pay to the person making it such remuneration and expenses as the Secretary of State may, with the approval of the Minister for the Civil Service, determine;

(b) in the case of an inquiry held by virtue of subsection (2)(b) above, may pay to the person holding it and to any assessor appointed to assist him such remuneration and expenses, and to persons attending the inquiry as witnesses such expenses, as the Secretary of State may, with the like approval, determine ; and

(c) may, to such extent as the Secretary of State may determine, defray the other costs, if any, of any such investigation and special report or inquiry.

(7) Where an inquiry is directed to be held by virtue of subsection (2)(b) above into any matter to which this section applies arising in Scotland, being a matter which causes the death of any person, no inquiry with regard to that death shall, unless the Lord Advocate otherwise directs, be held in pursuance of the Fatal Accidents Inquiry (Scotland) Act 1895.

Health and safety regulations and approved codes of practice

15 Health and safety regulations

(1) Subject to the provisions of section 50, the Secretary of State shall have power to make regulations under this section (in this part referred to as " health and safety regulations ") for any of the general purposes of this Part except as regards matters relating exclusively to agricultural operations.

(2) Without prejudice to the generality of the preceding subsection, health and safety regulations may for any of the general purposes of this Part make provision for any of the purposes mentioned in Schedule 3.

(3) Health and safety regulations—

(a) may repeal or modify any of the existing statutory provisions;

(b) may exclude or modify in relation to any specified class of case any of the provisions of sections 2 to 9 or any of the existing statutory provisions;

(c) may make a specified authority or class of authorities responsible, to such extent as may be specified, for the enforcement of any of the relevant statutory provisions.

(4) Health and safety regulations—

(a) may impose requirements by reference to the approval of the Commission or any other specified body or person;

(b) may provide for references in the regulations to any specified document to operate as references to that document as revised or re-issued from time to time.

(5) Health and safety regulations—

(a) may provide (either unconditionally or subject to conditions, and with or without limit of time) for exemptions from any requirement or prohibition imposed by or under any of the relevant statutory provisions;

(b) may enable exemptions from any requirement or prohibition imposed by or under any of the relevant statutory provisions to be granted (either unconditionally or subject to conditions, and with or without limit of time) by any specified person or by any person authorised in that behalf by a specified authority.

(6) Health and safety regulations—

(a) may specify the persons or classes of persons who, in the event of a contravention of a requirement or prohibition imposed by or under the regulations, are to be guilty of an offence, whether in addition to or to the exclusion of other persons or classes of persons;

(b) may provide for any specified defence to be available in proceedings for any offence under the relevant statutory provisions either generally or in specified circumstances;

(c) may exclude proceedings on indictment in relation to offences consisting of a contravention of a requirement or prohibition imposed by or under any of the existing statutory provisions, sections 2 to 9 or health and safety regulations;

(d) may restrict the punishments which can be imposed in respect of any such offence as is mentioned in paragraph (c) above.

(7) Without prejudice to section 35, health and safety regulations may make provision for enabling offences under any of the relevant statutory provisions to be treated as having been committed at any specified place for the purpose of bringing any such offence within the field of responsibility of any enforcing authority or conferring jurisdiction on any court to entertain proceedings for any such offence.

(8) Health and safety regulations may take the form of regulations applying to particular circumstances only or to a particular case only (for example, regulations applying to particular premises only).

(9) If an Order in Council is made under section 84(3) providing that this section shall apply to or in relation to persons, premises or work outside Great Britain then, notwithstanding the Order, health and safety regulations shall not apply to or in relation to aircraft in flight, vessels, hovercraft or offshore installations outside Great Britain or persons at work outside Great Britain in connection with submarine cables or submarine pipelines except in so far as the regulations expressly so provide.

(10) In this section " specified " means specified in health and safety regulations.

16 Approval of codes of practice by the Commission

(1) For the purpose of providing practical guidance with respect to the requirements of any provision of sections 2 to 7 or of health and safety regulations or of any of the existing statutory provisions, the Commission may, subject to the following subsection and except as regards matters relating exclusively to agricultural operations—

(a) approve and issue such codes of practice (whether prepared by it or not) as in its opinion are suitable for that purpose;

(b) approve such codes of practice issued or proposed to be issued otherwise than by the Commission as in its opinion are suitable for that purpose.

(2) The Commission shall not approve a code of practice under subsection (1) above without the consent of the Secretary of State, and shall, before seeking his consent, consult—

(a) any government department or other body that appears to the Commission to be appropriate (and, in particular, in the case of a code relating to electromagnetic radiations, the National Radiological Protection Board); and

(b) such government departments and other bodies, if any, as in relation to any matter dealt with in the code, the Commission is required to consult under this section by virtue of directions given to it by the Secretary of State.

(3) Where a code of practice is approved by the Commission under subsection (1) above, the Commission shall issue a notice in writing—

(a) identifying the code in question and stating the date on which its approval by the Commission is to take effect; and

(b) specifying for which of the provisions mentioned in subsection (1) above the code is approved.

(4) The Commission may—

(a) from time to time revise the whole or any part of any code of practice prepared by it in pursuance of this section;

(b) approve any revision or proposed revision of the whole or any part of any code of practice for the time being approved under this section ;

and the provisions of subsections (2) and (3) above shall, with the necessary modifications, apply in relation to the approval of any revision under this subsection as they apply in relation to the approval of a code of practice under subsection (1) above.

(5) The Commission may at any time with the consent of the Secretary of State withdraw its approval from any code of practice approved under this section, but before seeking his consent shall consult the same government departments and other bodies as it would be required to consult under subsection (2) above if it were proposing to approve the code.

(6) Where under the preceding subsection the Commission withdraws its approval from a code of practice approved under this section, the Commission shall issue a notice in writing identifying the code in question and stating the date on which its approval of it is to cease to have effect.

(7) References in this Part to an approved code of practice are references to that code as it has effect for the time being by virtue of any revision of the whole or any part of it approved under this section.

(8) The power of the Commission under subsection (1)(b) above to approve a code of practice issued or proposed to be issued otherwise than by the Commission shall include power to approve a part of such a code of practice; and accordingly in this Part "code of practice" may be read as including a part of such a code of practice.

17 Use of approved codes of practice in criminal proceedings

(1) A failure on the part of any person to observe any provision of an approved code of practice shall not of itself render him liable to any civil or criminal proceedings ; but where in any criminal proceedings a party is alleged to have committed an offence by reason of a contravention of any requirement or prohibition imposed by or under any such provision as is mentioned in section 16(1) being a provision for which there was an approved code of practice at the time of the alleged contravention, the following subsection shall have effect with respect to that code in relation to those proceedings.

(2) Any provision of the code of practice which appears to the court to be relevant to the requirement or prohibition alleged to have been contravened shall be admissible in evidence in the proceedings; and if it is proved that there was at any material time a failure to observe any provision of the code which appears to the court to be relevant to any matter which it is necessary for the prosecution to prove in order to establish a contravention of that requirement or prohibition, that matter shall be taken as proved unless the court is satisfied that the requirement or prohibition was in respect of that matter complied with otherwise than by way of observance of that provision of the code.

(3) In any criminal proceedings—

(a) a document purporting to be a notice issued by the Commission under section 16 shall be taken to be such a notice unless the contrary is proved; and

(b) a code of practice which appears to the court to be the subject of such a notice shall be taken to be the subject of that notice unless the contrary is proved.

Enforcement

18 Authorities responsible for enforcement of the relevant statutory provisions

(1) It shall be the duty of the Executive to make adequate arrangements for the enforcement of the relevant statutory provisions except to the extent that some other authority or class of authorities is by any of those provisions or by regulations under subsection (2) below made responsible for their enforcement.

(2) The Secretary of State may by regulations—

(a) make local authorities responsible for the enforcement of the relevant statutory provisions to such extent as may be prescribed;

(b) make provision for enabling responsibility for enforcing any of the relevant statutory provisions to be, to such extent as may be determined under the regulations-

(i) transferred from the Executive to local authorities or from local authorities to the Executive; or

(ii) assigned to the Executive or to local authorities for the purpose of removing any uncertainty as to what are by virtue of this subsection their respective responsibilities for the enforcement of those provisions:

and any regulations made in pursuance of paragraph (b) above shall include provision for securing that any transfer or assignment effected under the regulations is brought to the notice of persons affected by it.

(3) Any provision made by regulations under the preceding subsection shall have effect subject to any provision made by health and safety regulations or agricultural health and safety regulations in pursuance of section 15(3)(c).

(4) It shall be the duty of every local authority—

(a) to make adequate arrangements for the enforcement within their area of the relevant statutory provisions to the extent that they are by any of those provisions or by regulations under subsection (2) above made responsible for their enforcement; and

(b) to perform the duty imposed on them by the preceding paragraph and any other functions conferred on them by any of the relevant statutory provisions in accordance with such guidance as the Commission may give them.

(5) Where any authority other than the appropriate Agriculture Minister, the Executive or a local authority is by any of the relevant statutory provisions or by regulations under subsection (2) above made responsible for the enforcement of any of those provisions to any extent, it shall be the duty of that authority—

(a) to make adequate arrangements for the enforcement of those provisions to that extent; and

(b) to perform the duty imposed on the authority by the preceding paragraph and any other functions conferred on the authority by any of the relevant statutory provisions in accordance with such guidance as the Commission may give to the authority.

(6) Nothing in the provisions of this Act or of any regulations made thereunder charging any person in Scotland with the enforcement of any of the relevant statutory provisions shall be construed as authorising that person to institute proceedings for any offence.

(7) In this Part—

(a) "enforcing authority" means the Executive or any other authority which is by any of the relevant statutory provisions or by regulations under subsection (2) above made responsible for the enforcement of any of those provisions to any extent; and

(b) any reference to an enforcing authority's field of responsibility is a reference to the field over which that authority's responsibility for the enforcement of those provisions extends for the time being ;

but where by virtue of paragraph (a) of section 13(1) the performance of any function of the Commission or the Executive is delegated to a government department or person, references to the Commission or the Executive (or to an enforcing authority where that authority is the Executive) in any provision of this Part which relates to that function shall, so far as may be necessary to give effect to any agreement under that paragraph, be construed as references to that department or person; and accordingly any reference to the field of responsibility of an enforcing authority shall be construed as a reference to the field over which that department or person for the time being performs such a function.

19 Appointment of inspectors

(1) Every enforcing authority may appoint as inspectors (under whatever title it may from time to time determine) such persons having suitable qualifications as it thinks necessary for carrying into effect the relevant statutory provisions within its field of responsibility, and may terminate any appointment made under this section.

(2) Every appointment of a person as an inspector under this section shall be made by an instrument in writing specifying which of the powers conferred on inspectors by the relevant statutory provisions are to be exercisable by the person appointed; and an inspector shall in right of his appointment under this section—

(a) be entitled to exercise only such of those powers as are so specified ; and

(b) be entitled to exercise the powers so specified only within the field of responsibility of the authority which appointed him.

(3) So much of an inspector's instrument of appointment as specifies the powers which he is entitled to exercise may be varied by the enforcing authority which appointed him.

(4) An inspector shall, if so required when exercising or seeking to exercise any power conferred on him by any of the relevant statutory provisions, produce his instrument of appointment or a duly authenticated copy thereof.

20 Powers of inspectors

(1) Subject to the provisions of section 19 and this section, an inspector may, for the purpose of carrying into effect any of the relevant statutory provisions within the field of responsibility of the enforcing authority which appointed him, exercise the powers set out in subsection (2) below.

(2) The powers of an inspector referred to in the preceding subsection are the following, namely—

(a) at any reasonable time (or, in a situation which in his opinion is or may be dangerous, at any time) to enter any premises which he has reason co believe it is necessary for him to enter for the purpose mentioned in subsection (1) above ;

(b) to take with him a constable if he has reasonable cause to apprehend any serious obstruction in the execution of his duty;

(c) without prejudice to the preceding paragraph, on entering any premises by virtue of paragraph (a) above to take with him—

(i) any other person duly authorised by his (the inspector's) enforcing authority ; and

(ii) any equipment or materials required for any purpose for which the power of entry is being exercised;

(d) to make such examination and investigation as may in any circumstances be necessary for the purpose mentioned in subsection (1) above ;

(e) as regards any premises which he has power to enter, to direct that those premises or any part of them, or anything therein, shall be left undisturbed (whether generally or in particular respects) for so long as is reasonably necessary for the purpose of any examination or investigation under paragraph (d) above;

(f) to take such measurements and photographs and make such recordings as he considers necessary for the purpose of any examination or investigation under paragraph (d) above;

(g) to take samples of any articles or substances found in any premises which he has power to enter, and of the atmosphere in or in the vicinity of any such premises ;

(h) in the case of any article or substance found in any premises which he has power to enter, being an article or substance which appears to him to have caused or to be likely to cause danger to health or safety, to cause it to be dismantled or subjected to any process or test (but not so as to damage or destroy it unless this is in the circumstances necessary for the purpose mentioned in subsection (1) above);

(i) in the case of any such article or substance as is mentioned in the preceding paragraph, to take possession of it and detain it for so long as is necessary for all or any of the following purposes, namely—

(i) to examine it and do to it anything which he has power to do under that paragraph ;

(ii) to ensure that it is not tampered with before his examination of it is completed ;

(iii) to ensure that it is available for use as evidence in any proceedings for an offence under any of the relevant statutory provisions or any proceedings relating to a notice under section 21 or 22;

(j) to require any person whom he has reasonable cause to believe to be able to give any information relevant to any examination or investigation under paragraph (d) above to answer (in the absence of persons other than a person nominated by him to be present and any persons whom the inspector may allow to be present) such questions as the inspector thinks fit to ask and to sign a declaration of the truth of his answers ;

(k) to require the production of, inspect, and take copies of or of any entry in—

(i) any books or documents which by virtue of any of the relevant statutory provisions are required to be kept; and

(ii) any other books or documents which it is necessary for him to see for the purposes of any examination or investigation under paragraph (d) above;

(l) to require any person to afford him such facilities and assistance with respect to any matters or things within that person's control or in relation to which that person has responsibilities as are necessary to enable the inspector to exercise any of the powers conferred on him by this section ;

(m) any other power which is necessary for the purpose mentioned in subsection (1) above.

(3) The Secretary of State may by regulations make provision as to the procedure to be followed in connection with the taking of samples under subsection (2)(g) above (including provision as to the way in which samples that have been so taken are to be dealt with).

(4) Where an inspector proposes to exercise the power conferred by subsection (2)(h) above in the case of an article or substance found in any premises, he shall, if so requested by a person who at the time is present in and has responsibilities in relation to those premises, cause anything which is to be done by virtue of that power to be done in the presence of that person unless the inspector considers that its being done in that person's presence would be prejudicial to the safety of the State.

(5) Before exercising the power conferred by subsection (2)(h) above in the case of any article or substance, an inspector shall consult such persons as appear to him appropriate for the purpose of ascertaining what dangers, if any, there may be in doing anything which he proposes to do under that power.

(6) Where under the power conferred by subsection (2)(i) above an inspector takes possession of any article or substance found in any premises, he shall leave there, either with a responsible person or, if that is impracticable, fixed in a conspicuous position, a notice giving particulars of that article or substance sufficient to identify it and stating that he has taken possession of it under that power; and before taking possession of any such substance under that power an inspector shall, if it is practicable for him to do so, take a sample thereof and give to a responsible person at the premises a portion of the sample marked in a manner sufficient to identify it.

(7) No answer given by a person in pursuance of a requirement imposed under subsection (2)(j) above shall be admissible in evidence against that person or the husband or wife of that person in any proceedings.

(8) Nothing in this section shall be taken to compel the production by any person of a document of which he would on grounds of legal professional privilege be entitled to withhold production on an order for discovery in an action in the High Court or, as the case may be, on an order for the production of documents in an action in the Court of Session.

21 Improvement notices

If an inspector is of the opinion that a person—

(a) is contravening one or more of the relevant statutory provisions; or

(b) has contravened one or more of those provisions in circumstances that make it likely that the contravention will continue or be repeated,

he may serve on him a notice (in this Part referred to as " an improvement notice ") stating that he is of that opinion, specifying the provision or provisions as to which he is of that opinion, giving particulars of the reasons why he is of that opinion, and requiring that person to remedy the contravention or, as the case may be, the matters occasioning it within such period (ending not earlier than the period within which an appeal against the notice can be brought under section 24) as may be specified in the notice.

22 Prohibition notices

(1) This section applies to any activities which are being or are about to be carried on by or under the control of any person, being activities to or in relation to which any of the relevant statutory provisions apply or will, if the activities are so carried on, apply.

(2) If as regards any activities to which this section applies an inspector is of the opinion that, as carried on or about to be carried on by or under the control of the person in

question, the activities involve or, as the case may be, will involve a risk of serious personal injury, the inspector may serve on that person a notice (in this Part referred to as " a prohibition notice ").

(3) A prohibition notice shall—

(a) state that the inspector is of the said opinion ;

(b) specify the matters which in his opinion give or, as the case may be, will give rise to the said risk ;

(c) where in his opinion any of those matters involves or, as the case may be, will involve a contravention of any of the relevant statutory provisions, state that he is of that opinion, specify the provision or provisions as to which he is of that opinion, and give particulars of the reasons why he is of that opinion ; and

(d) direct that the activities to which the notice relates shall not be carried on by or under the control of the person on whom the notice is served unless the matters specified in the notice in pursuance of paragraph (b) above and any associated contraventions of provisions so specified in pursuance of paragraph (c) above have been remedied.

(4) A direction given in pursuance of subsection (3)(d) above shall take immediate effect if the inspector is of the opinion, and states it, that the risk of serious personal injury is or, as the case may be, will be imminent, and shall have effect at the end of a period specified in the notice in any other case.

23 Provisions supplementary to ss. 21 and 22

(1) In this section " a notice " means an improvement notice or a prohibition notice.

(2) A notice may (but need not) include directions as to the measures to be taken to remedy any contravention or matter to which the notice relates ; and any such directions—

(a) may be framed to any extent by reference to any approved code of practice ; and

(b) may be framed so as to afford the person on whom the notice is served a choice between different ways of remedying the contravention or matter.

(3) Where any of the relevant statutory provisions applies to a building or any matter connected with a building and an inspector proposes to serve an improvement notice relating to a contravention of that provision in connection with that building or matter, the notice shall not direct any measures to be taken to remedy the contravention of that provision which are more onerous than those necessary to secure conformity with the requirements of any building regulations for the time being in force to which that building or matter would be required to conform if the relevant building were being newly erected unless the provision in question imposes specific requirements more onerous than the requirements of any such building regulations to which the building or matter would be required to conform as aforesaid.

In this subsection " the relevant building ", in the case of a building, means that building, and, in the case of a matter connected with a building, means the building with which the matter is connected.

(4) Before an inspector serves in connection with any premises used or about to be used as a place of work a notice requiring or likely to lead to the taking of measures affecting the means of escape in case of fire with which the premises are or ought to be provided, he shall consult the fire authority.

In this subsection " fire authority " has the meaning assigned by section 43(1) of the Fire Precautions Act 1971.

(5) Where an improvement notice or a prohibition notice which is not to take immediate effect has been served—

(a) the notice may be withdrawn by an inspector at any time before the end of the period specified therein in pursuance of section 21 or section 22(4) as the case may be; and

(b) the period so specified may be extended or further extended by an inspector at any time when an appeal against the notice is not pending.

(6) In the application of this section to Scotland—

(a) in subsection (3) for the words from " with the requirements " to " aforesaid " there shall be substituted the words—

"(a) to any provisions of the building standards regulations to which that building or matter would be required to conform if the relevant building were being newly erected ; or

(b) where the sheriff, on an appeal to him under section 16 of the Building (Scotland) Act 1959—

(i) against an order under section 10 of that Act requiring the execution of operations necessary to make the building or matter conform to the building standards regulations, or

(ii) against an order under section 11 of that Act requiring the building or matter to conform to a provision of such regulations, has varied the order, to any provisions of the building standards regulations referred to in paragraph (a) above as affected by the order as so varied, unless the relevant statutory provision imposes specific requirements more onerous than the requirements of any provisions of building standards regulations as aforesaid or, as the case may be, than the requirements of the order as varied by the sheriff.";

(b) after subsection (5) there shall be inserted the following subsection—

"(5A) In subsection (3) above ' building standards regulations' has the same meaning as in section 3 of the Building (Scotland) Act 1959.".

24 Appeal against improvement or prohibition notice

(1) In this section " a notice " means an improvement notice or a prohibition notice.

(2) A person on whom a notice is served may within such period from the date of its service as may be prescribed appeal to an industrial tribunal; and on such an appeal the tribunal may either cancel or affirm the notice and, if it affirms it, may do so either in its original form or with such modifications as the tribunal may in the circumstances think fit,

(3) Where an appeal under this section is brought against a notice within the period allowed under the preceding subsection, then—

(a) in the case of an improvement notice, the bringing of the appeal shall have the effect of suspending the operation of the notice until the appeal is finally disposed of or, if the appeal is withdrawn, until the withdrawal of the appeal;

(b) in the case of a prohibition notice, the bringing of the appeal shall have the like effect if, but only if, on the application of the appellant the tribunal so directs (and then only from the giving of the direction).

(4) One or more assessors may be appointed for the purposes of any proceedings brought before an industrial tribunal under this section.

25 Power to deal with cause of imminent danger

(1) Where, in the case of any article or substance found by him in any premises which he has power to enter, an inspector has reasonable cause to believe that, in the circumstances in which he finds it, the article or substance is a cause of imminent danger of serious personal injury, he may seize it and cause it to be rendered harmless (whether by destruction or otherwise).

(2) Before there is rendered harmless under this section—

(a) any article that forms part of a batch of similar articles ; or

(b) any substance,

the inspector shall, if it is practicable for him to do so, take a sample thereof and give to a responsible person at the premises where the article or substance was found by him a portion of the sample marked in a manner sufficient to identify it.

(3) As soon as may be after any article or substance has been seized and rendered harmless under this section, the inspector shall prepare and sign a written report giving particulars of the circumstances in which the article or substance was seized and so dealt with by him, and shall—

(a) give a signed copy of the report to a responsible person at the premises where the article or substance was found by him; and

(b) unless that person is the owner of the article or substance, also serve a signed copy of the report on the owner;

and if, where paragraph (b) above applies, the inspector cannot after reasonable enquiry ascertain the name or address of the owner, the copy may be served on him by giving it to the person to whom a copy was given under the preceding paragraph.

26 Power of enforcing authorities to indemnify their inspectors

Where an action has been brought against an inspector in respect of an act done in the execution or purported execution of any of the relevant statutory provisions and the circumstances are such that he is not legally entitled to require the enforcing authority which appointed him to indemnify him, that authority may, nevertheless, indemnify him against the whole or part of any damages and costs or expenses which he may have been ordered to pay or may have incurred, if the authority is satisfied that he honestly believed that the act complained of was within his powers and that his duty as an inspector required or entitled him to do it.

Obtaining and disclosure of information

27 Obtaining of information by the Commission, the Executive, enforcing authorities etc.

(1) For the purpose of obtaining—

(a) any information which the Commission needs for the discharge of its functions; or

(b) any information which an enforcing authority needs for the discharge of the authority's functions,

the Commission may, with the consent of the Secretary of State, serve on any person a notice requiring that person to furnish to the Commission or, as the case may be, to the enforcing authority in question such information about such matters as may be specified in the notice, and to do so in such form and manner and within such time as may be so specified.

In this subsection " consent" includes a general consent extending to cases of any stated description.

(2) Nothing in section 9 of the Statistics of Trade Act 1947 (which restricts the disclosure of information obtained under that Act) shall prevent or penalise—

(a) the disclosure by a Minister of the Crown to the Commission or the Executive of information obtained under that Act about any undertaking within the meaning of that Act, being information consisting of the names and addresses of the persons carrying on the undertaking, the nature of the undertaking's activities, the numbers of persons of different descriptions who work in the undertaking, the addresses or places where activities of the undertaking are or were carried on, the nature of the activities carried on there, or the numbers of persons of different descriptions who work or worked in the undertaking there ; or

(b) the disclosure by the Manpower Services Commission, the Employment Service Agency or the Training Services Agency to the Commission or the Executive of information so obtained which is of a kind specified in a notice in writing given to the disclosing body and the recipient of the information by the Secretary of State under this paragraph.

(3) In the preceding subsection any reference to a Minister of the Crown, the Commission, the Executive, the Manpower Services Commission or either of the said Agencies includes respectively a reference to an officer of his or of that body and also, in the case of a reference to the Commission, includes a reference to—

(a) a person performing any functions of the Commission or the Executive on its behalf by virtue of section 13(1)(a);

(b) an officer of a body which is so performing any such functions ; and

(c) an adviser appointed in pursuance of section 13(1)(d).

(4) A person to whom information is disclosed in pursuance of subsection (2) above shall not use the information for a purpose other than a purpose of the Commission or, as the case may be, of the Executive.

28 Restrictions on disclosure of information

(1) In this and the two following subsections—

(a) " relevant information" means information obtained by a person under section 27(1) or furnished to any person in pursuance of a requirement imposed by any of the relevant statutory provisions; and

(b) " the recipient ", in relation to any relevant information, means the person by whom that information was so obtained or to whom that information was so furnished, as the case may be.

(2) Subject to the following subsection, no relevant information shall be disclosed without the consent of the person by whom it was furnished.

(3) The preceding subsection shall not apply to—

(a) disclosure of information to the Commission, the Executive, a government department or any enforcing authority;

(b) without prejudice to paragraph (a) above, disclosure by the recipient of information to any person for the purpose of any function conferred on the recipient by or under any of the relevant statutory provisions;

(c) without prejudice to paragraph (a) above, disclosure by the recipient of information to—

(i) an officer of a local authority who is authorised by that authority to receive it,

(ii) an officer of a water authority or water development board who is authorised by that authority or board to receive it,

(iii) an officer of a river purification board who is authorised by that board to receive it, or

(iv) a constable authorised by a chief officer of police to receive it;

(d) disclosure by the recipient of information in a form calculated to prevent it from being identified as relating to a particular person or case ;

(e) disclosure of information for the purposes of any legal proceedings or any investigation or inquiry held by virtue of section 14(2), or for the purposes of a report of any such proceedings or inquiry or of a special report made by virtue of section 14(2).

(4) In the preceding subsection any reference to the Commission, the Executive, a government department or an enforcing authority includes respectively a reference to an officer of that body or authority (including, in the case of an enforcing authority, any inspector appointed by it), and also, in the case of a reference to the Commission, includes a reference to—

(a) a person performing any functions of the Commission or the Executive on its behalf by virtue of section 13(1)(a);

(b) an officer of a body which is so performing any such functions; and

(c) an adviser appointed in pursuance of section 13(1)(d).

(5) A person to whom information is disclosed in pursuance of subsection (3) above shall not use the information for a purpose other than—

(a) in a case falling within paragraph (a) of that subsection, a purpose of the Commission or of the Executive or of the government department in question, or the purposes of the enforcing authority in question in connection with the relevant statutory provisions, as the case may be;

(b) in the case of information given to an officer of a local authority or of a water authority or of a river purification board or water development board, the purposes of the authority or board in connection with the relevant statutory provisions or any enactment whatsoever relating to public health, public safety or the protection of the environment;

(c) in the case of information given to a constable, the purposes of the police in connection with the relevant statutory provisions or any enactment whatsoever relating to public health, public safety or the safety of the State.

(6) In subsections (3)(c) and (5) above, before 16th May 1975, the references to a water authority in their application to Scotland shall be construed as references to a regional water board.

(7) A person shall not disclose any information obtained by him as a result of the exercise of any power conferred by section 14(4)(a) or 20 (including, in particular, any information with respect to any trade secret obtained by him in any premises entered by him by virtue of any such power) except—

(a) for the purposes of his functions; or

(b) for the purposes of any legal proceedings or any investigation or inquiry held by virtue of section 14(2) or for the purposes of a report of any such proceedings or inquiry or of a special report made by virtue of section 14(2); or

(c) with the relevant consent.

In this subsection " the relevant consent" means, in the case of information furnished in pursuance of a requirement imposed under section 20, the consent of the person who furnished it, and, in any other case, the consent of a person having responsibilities in relation to the premises where the information was obtained.

(8) Notwithstanding anything in the preceding subsection an inspector shall, in circumstances in which it is necessary to do so for the purpose of assisting in keeping persons (or the representatives of persons) employed at any premises adequately informed about matters affecting their health, safety and welfare, give to such persons or their representatives the following descriptions of information, that is to say—

(a) factual information obtained by him as mentioned in that subsection which relates to those premises or anything which was or is therein or was or is being done therein; and

(b) information with respect to any action which he has taken or proposes to take in or in connection with those premises in the performance of his functions;

and, where an inspector does as aforesaid, he shall give the like information to the employer of the first-mentioned persons.

Special provisions relating to agriculture

29 General functions of Ministers responsible for agriculture in relation to the relevant agricultural purposes

(1) It shall be the duty of the appropriate Agriculture Minister—

(a) to do such things and make such arrangements as he considers appropriate for the relevant agricultural purposes; and

(b) to make such arrangements as he considers appropriate for securing that employers, employees, organisations representing employers and employees respectively, and other persons concerned with matters relevant to any of those purposes are kept informed of, and adequately advised on, such matters.

(2) The Minister of Agriculture, Fisheries and Food shall make an annual report to Parliament of his proceedings under the relevant statutory provisions, and may include that report in the annual report made to Parliament in pursuance of section 13 of the Agricultural Wages Act 1948.

(3) The Secretary of State concerned with agriculture in Scotland shall make an annual report to Parliament of his proceedings under the relevant statutory provisions.

30 Agricultural health and safety regulations

(1) Regulations under this section (in this Part referred to as " agricultural health and safety regulations".) may be made for any of the relevant agricultural purposes.

(2) Agricultural health and safety regulations may be either regulations applying to Great Britain and made by the Minister of Agriculture, Fisheries and Food and the Secretary of State acting jointly, or regulations applying to England and Wales only and made by the said Minister, or regulations applying to Scotland only and made by the Secretary of State.

(3) Where health and safety regulations make provision for any purpose with respect to a matter that relates to (but not exclusively to) agricultural operations—

(a) provision for that purpose shall not be made with respect to that matter by agricultural health and safety regulations so as to have effect while the first-mentioned provision is in force except for the purpose of imposing requirements additional to those imposed by health and safety regulations, being additional requirements which in the opinion of the authority making the agricultural health and safety regulations are necessary or expedient in the special circumstances of agricultural operations; and

(b) in the event of any inconsistency between the first-mentioned provision and any provision made with respect to that matter by agricultural health and safety regulations, the first-mentioned provision shall prevail.

(4) The provisions of section 15(2) to (10) and Schedule 3 shall have effect in relation to agricultural health and safety regulations as they have effect in relation to health and safety regulations subject to the following modifications, that is to say—

(a) references to the relevant statutory provisions or the existing statutory provisions shall be read as references to such of those provisions as relate to agriculture;

(b) in section 15(4) the references to the Commission shall be read as references to the appropriate Agriculture Minister;

(c) in section 15(6) and (10) and paragraph 23 of Schedule 3, the reference to health and safety regulations shall be read as a reference to agricultural health and safety regulations.

(5) Without prejudice to the generality of subsection (1) above, agricultural health and safety regulations may, as regards agricultural licences under any of the relevant statutory provisions, make provision for requiring the authority having power to issue, renew, vary, transfer or revoke such licences to notify—

(a) any applicant for the issue, renewal, variation or transfer of such a licence of any proposed decision of the authority to refuse the application ; or

(b) the holder of such a licence of any proposed decision of the authority to revoke the licence or to vary any term, condition or restriction on or subject to which the licence is held ;

and for enabling persons aggrieved by any such proposed decision to make representations to, or to a person appointed by, the relevant authority within the period and in the manner prescribed by the regulations.

(6) In relation to any agricultural health and safety regulations made in pursuance of paragraph 2 of Schedule 3 as applied by this section, subsection (2) above shall have effect as if after the words " Great Britain " there were inserted the words " or the United Kingdom ".

31 Enforcement of the relevant statutory provisions in connection with agriculture

Subject to any provision made by regulations under section 15, 18 or 30, it shall be the duty of the appropriate Agriculture Minister to make adequate arrangements for the enforcement of the relevant statutory provisions in their application to matters relating exclusively to the relevant agricultural purposes.

32 Application of provisions of this Part in connection with agriculture

(1) The following provisions of this section shall have effect with a view to the application of certain provisions of this Part in relation to the Agriculture Ministers or matters relating exclusively to the relevant agricultural purposes.

(2) Subject to the following subsection—

(a) sections 13, 14, 17(3), 27 and 28 shall apply in relation to the appropriate Agriculture Minister as they apply in relation to the Commission ;

(b) section 16 shall apply in relation to matters relating exclusively to the relevant agricultural purposes as it applies in relation to other matters.

(3) In their application as provided by the preceding subsection, the provisions of this Part which are specified in the first column of Schedule 4 shall have effect subject to the modifications provided for in the second column of that Schedule.

Provisions as to offences

33 Offences

(1) It is an offence for a person—

(a) to fail to discharge a duty to which he is subject by virtue of sections 2 to 7 ;

(b) to contravene section 8 or 9 ;

(c) to contravene any health and safety regulations or agricultural health and safety regulations or any requirement or prohibition imposed under any such regulations (including any requirement or prohibition to which he is subject by virtue of the terms of or any condition or restriction attached to any licence, approval, exemption or other authority issued, given or granted under the regulations);

(d) to contravene any requirement imposed by or under regulations under section 14 or intentionally to obstruct any person in the exercise of his powers under that section;

(e) to contravene any requirement imposed by an inspector under section 20 or 25 ;

(f) to prevent or attempt to prevent any other person from appearing before an inspector or from answering any question to which an inspector may by virtue of section 20(2) require an answer ;

(g) to contravene any requirement or prohibition imposed by an improvement notice or a prohibition notice (including any such notice as modified on appeal);

(h) intentionally to obstruct an inspector in the exercise or performance of his powers or duties ;

(i) to contravene any requirement imposed by a notice under section 27(1);

(j) to use or disclose any information in contravention of section 27(4) or 28 ;

(k) to make a statement which he knows to be false or recklessly to make a statement which is false where the statement is made—

(i) in purported compliance with a requirement to furnish any information imposed by or under any of the relevant statutory provisions; or

(ii) for the purpose of obtaining the issue of a document under any of the relevant statutory provisions to himself or another person ;

(l) intentionally to make a false entry in any register, book, notice or other document required by or under any of the relevant statutory provisions to be kept, served or given or, with intent to deceive, to make use of any such entry which he knows to be false ;

(m) with intent to deceive, to forge or use a document issued or authorised to be issued under any of the relevant statutory provisions or required for any purpose thereunder or to make or have in his possession a document so closely resembling any such document as to be calculated to deceive;

(n) falsely to pretend to be an inspector ;

(o) to fail to comply with an order made by a court under section 42.

(2) A person guilty of an offence under paragraph (d). (f), (h) or (n) of subsection (1) above, or of an offence under paragraph (e) of that subsection consisting of contravening a requirement imposed by an inspector under section 20, shall be liable on summary conviction to a fine not exceeding £400.

(3) Subject to any provision made by virtue of section 15(6)(d) or by virtue of paragraph 2(2) of Schedule 3, a person guilty of an offence under any paragraph of subsection (1) above not mentioned in the preceding subsection, or of an offence under subsection (1) (e) above not falling within the preceding subsection, or of an offence under any of the existing statutory provisions, being an offence for which no other penalty is specified, shall be liable—

(a) on summary conviction, to a fine not exceeding £400;

(b) on conviction on indictment—

(i) if the offence is one to which this sub-paragraph applies, to imprisonment for a term not exceeding two years, or a fine, or both ;

(ii) if the offence is not one to which the preceding sub-paragraph applies, to a fine.

(4) Subsection (3)(b)(i) above applies to the following offences—

(a) an offence consisting of contravening any of the relevant statutory provisions by doing otherwise than under the authority of a licence issued by the

Executive or the appropriate Agriculture Minister something for the doing of which such a licence is necessary under the relevant statutory provisions;

(b) an offence consisting of contravening a term of or a condition or restriction attached to any such licence as is mentioned in the preceding paragraph;

(c) an offence consisting of acquiring or attempting to acquire, possessing or using an explosive article or substance (within the meaning of any of the relevant statutory provisions) in contravention of any of the relevant statutory provisions;

(d) an offence under subsection (Dig) above consisting of contravening a requirement or prohibition imposed by a prohibition notice ;

(e) an offence under subsection (1)(j) above.

(5) Where a person is convicted of an offence under subsection (1)(g) or (o) above, then, if the contravention in respect of which he was convicted is continued after the conviction he shall (subject to section 42(3)) be guilty of a further offence and liable in respect thereof to a fine not exceeding £50 for each day on which the contravention is so continued.

(6) In this section " forge " has, for England and Wales, the same meaning as in the Forgery Act 1913.

34 Extension of time for bringing summary proceedings

(1) Where—

(a) a special report on any matter to which section 14 of this Act applies is made by virtue of subsection (2) to) of that section ; or

(b) a report is made by the person holding an inquiry into any such matter by virtue of subsection (2) (b) of that section; or

(c) a coroner's inquest is held touching the death of any person whose death may have been caused by an accident which happened while he was at work or by a disease which he contracted or probably contracted at work or by any accident, act or omission which occurred in connection with the work of any person whatsoever; or

(d) a public inquiry into any death that may have been so caused is held under the Fatal Accidents Inquiry (Scotland) Act 1895 or the Fatal Accidents and Sudden Deaths Inquiry (Scotland) Act 1906,

and it appears from the report or, in a case falling within paragraph (c) or (d) above, from the proceedings at the inquest or inquiry, that any of the relevant statutory provisions was contravened at a time which is material in relation to the subject-matter of the report, inquest or inquiry, summary proceedings against any person liable to be proceeded against in respect of the contravention may be commenced at any time within three months of the making of the report or, in a case falling within paragraph (c) or (d) above, within three months of the conclusion of the inquest or inquiry.

(2) Where an offence under any of the relevant statutory provisions is committed by reason of a failure to do something at or within a time fixed by or under any of those provisions, the offence shall be deemed to continue until that thing is done.

(3) Summary proceedings for an offence to which this subsection applies may be commenced at any time within six months from the date on which there comes to the knowledge of a responsible enforcing authority evidence sufficient in the opinion of

that authority to justify a prosecution for that offence ; and for the purposes of this subsection—

(a) a certificate of an enforcing authority stating that such evidence came to its knowledge on a specified date shall be conclusive evidence of that fact; and

(b) a document purporting to be such a certificate and to be signed by or on behalf of the enforcing authority in question shall be presumed to be such a certificate unless the contrary is proved.

(4) The preceding subsection applies to any offence under any of the relevant statutory provisions which a person commits by virtue of any provision or requirement to which he is subject as the designer, manufacturer, importer or supplier of any thing ; and in that subsection " responsible enforcing authority " means an enforcing authority within whose field of responsibility the offence in question lies, whether by virtue of section 35 or otherwise.

(5) In the application of subsection (3) above to Scotland—

(a) for the words from " there comes " to " that offence " there shall be substituted the words " evidence, sufficient in the opinion of the enforcing authority to justify a report to the Lord Advocate with a view to consideration of the question of prosecution, comes to the knowledge of the authority ";

(b) at the end of paragraph (b) there shall be added the words "and

(c) section 23(2) of the Summary Jurisdiction (Scotland) Act 1954 (date of commencement of proceedings) shall have effect as it has effect for the purposes of that section.".

35 Venue

An offence under any of the relevant statutory provisions committed in connection with any plant or substance may, if necessary for the purpose of bringing the offence within the field of responsibility of any enforcing authority or conferring jurisdiction on any court to entertain proceedings for the offence, be treated as having been committed at the place where that plant or substance is for the time being.

36 Offences due to fault of other person

(1) Where the commission by any person of an offence under any of the relevant statutory provisions is due to the act or default of some other person, that other person shall be guilty of the offence, and a person may be charged with and convicted of the offence by virtue of this subsection whether or not proceedings are taken against the first-mentioned person.

(2) Where there would be or have been the commission of an offence under section 33 by the Crown but for the circumstance that that section does not bind the Crown, and that fact is due to the act or default of a person other than the Crown, that person shall be guilty of the offence which, but for that circumstance, the Crown would be committing or would have committed, and may be charged with and convicted of that offence accordingly.

(3) The preceding provisions of this section are subject to any provision made by virtue of section 15(6).

37 Offences by bodies corporate

(1) Where an offence under any of the relevant statutory provisions committed by a body corporate is proved to have been committed with the consent or connivance of, or to have been attributable to any neglect on the part of, any director, manager, secretary or other similar officer of the body corporate or a person who was purporting to act in any such capacity, he as well as the body corporate shall be guilty of that offence and shall be liable to be proceeded against and punished accordingly.

(2) Where the affairs of a body corporate are managed by its members, the preceding subsection shall apply in relation to the acts and defaults of a member in connection with his functions of management as if he were a director of the body corporate.

38 Restriction on institution of proceedings in England and Wales

Proceedings for an offence under any of the relevant statutory provisions shall not, in England and Wales, be instituted except by an inspector or by or with the consent of the Director of Public Prosecutions.

39 Prosecutions by inspectors

(1) An inspector, if authorised in that behalf by the enforcing authority which appointed him, may, although not of counsel or a solicitor, prosecute before a magistrates' court proceedings for an offence under any of the relevant statutory provisions.

(2) This section shall not apply to Scotland.

40 Onus of proving limits of what is practicable etc.

In any proceedings for an offence under any of the relevant statutory provisions consisting of a failure to comply with a duty or requirement to do something so far as is practicable or so far as is reasonably practicable, or to use the best practicable means to do something, it shall be for the accused to prove (as the case may be) that it was not practicable or not reasonably practicable to do more than was in fact done to satisfy the duty or requirement, or that there was no better practicable means than was in fact used to satisfy the duty or requirement.

41 Evidence

(1) Where an entry is required by any of the relevant statutory provisions to be made in any register or other record, the entry, if made, shall, as against the person by or on whose behalf it was made, be admissible as evidence or in Scotland sufficient evidence of the facts stated therein.

(2) Where an entry which is so required to be so made with respect to the observance of any of the relevant statutory provisions has not been made, that fact shall be admissible as evidence or in Scotland sufficient evidence that that provision has not been observed.

42 Power of court to order cause of offence to be remedied or, in certain cases, forfeiture

(1) Where a person is convicted of an offence under any of the relevant statutory provisions in respect of any matters which appear to the court to be matters which it is in his power to remedy, the court may, in addition to or instead of imposing any punishment, order him, within such time as may be fixed by the order, to take such steps as may be specified in the order for remedying the said matters.

(2) The time fixed by an order under subsection (1) above may be extended or further extended by order of the court on an application made before the end of that time as originally fixed or as extended under this subsection, as the case may be.

(3) Where a person is ordered under subsection (1) above to remedy any matters, that person shall not be liable under any of the relevant statutory provisions in respect of those matters in so far as they continue during the time fixed by the order or any further time allowed under subsection (2) above.

(4) Subject to the following subsection, the court by or before which a person is convicted of an offence such as is mentioned in section 33(4)(c) in respect of any such explosive article or substance as is there mentioned may order the article or substance in question to be forfeited and either destroyed or dealt with in such other manner as the court may order.

(5) The court shall not order anything to be forfeited under the preceding subsection where a person claiming to be the owner of or otherwise interested in it applies to be heard by the court, unless an opportunity has been given to him to show cause why the order should not be made.

Financial provisions

43 Financial provisions

(1) It shall be the duty of the Secretary of State to pay to the Commission such sums as are approved by the Treasury and as he considers appropriate for the purpose of enabling the Commission to perform its functions; and it shall be the duty of the Commission to pay to the Executive such sums as the Commission considers appropriate for the purpose of enabling the Executive to perform its functions.

(2) Regulations may provide for such fees as may be fixed by or determined under the regulations to be payable for or in connection with the performance by or on behalf of any authority to which this subsection applies of any function conferred on that authority by or under any of the relevant statutory provisions.

(3) Subsection (2) above applies to the following authorities, namely the Commission, the Executive, the Secretary of State, the Minister of Agriculture, Fisheries and Food, every enforcing authority, and any other person on whom any function is conferred by or under any of the relevant statutory provisions.

(4) Regulations under this section may specify the person by whom any fee payable under the regulations is to be paid; but no such fee shall be made payable by a person in any of the following capacities, namely an employee, a person seeking employment, a person training for employment, and a person seeking training for employment.

(5) Without prejudice to section 82(3), regulations under this section may fix or provide for the determination of different fees in relation to different functions, or in relation to the same function in different circumstances.

(6) The power to make regulations under this section shall be exercisable—

(a) as regards functions with respect to matters not relating exclusively to agricultural operations, by the Secretary of State;

(b) as regards functions with respect to matters relating exclusively to the relevant agricultural purposes, by the appropriate argicultural authority.

(7) Regulations under this section as regards functions falling within subsection (6)(b) above may be either regulations applying to Great Britain and made by the Minister of Agriculture, Fisheries and Food and the Secretary of State acting jointly, or regulations applying to England and Wales only and made by the said Minister, or regulations applying to Scotland only and made by the Secretary of State; and in subsection (6)(b) above " the appropriate agricultural authority" shall be construed accordingly.

(8) In subsection (4) above the references to a person training for employment and a person seeking training for employment shall include respectively a person attending an industrial rehabilitation course provided by virtue of the Employment and Training Act 1973 and a person seeking to attend such a course.

(9) For the purposes of this section the performance by an inspector of his functions shall be treated as the performance by the enforcing authority which appointed him of functions conferred on that authority by or under any of the relevant statutory provisions.

Miscellaneous and supplementary

44 Appeals in connection with licensing provisions in the relevant statutory provisions

(1) Any person who is aggrieved by a decision of an authority having power to issue licences (other than agricultural licences and nuclear site licences) under any of the relevant statutory provisions—

(a) refusing to issue him a licence, to renew a licence held by him, or to transfer to him a licence held by another;

(b) issuing him a licence on or subject to any term, condition or restriction whereby he is aggrieved ;

(c) varying or refusing to vary any term, condition or restriction on or subject to which a licence is held by him; or

(d) revoking a licence held by him,

may appeal to the Secretary of State.

(2) The Secretary of State may, in such cases as he considers it appropriate to do so, having regard to the nature of the questions which appear to him to arise, direct that an appeal under this section shall be determined on his behalf by a person appointed by him for that purpose.

(3) Before the determination of an appeal the Secretary of State shall ask the appellant and the authority against whose decision the appeal is brought whether they wish to appear and be heard on the appeal and—

(a) the appeal may be determined without a hearing of the parties if both of them express a wish not to appear and be heard as aforesaid ;

(b) the Secretary of State shall, if either of the parties expresses a wish to appear and be heard, afford to both of them an opportunity of so doing.

(4) The Tribunals and Inquiries Act 1971 shall apply to a hearing held by a person appointed in pursuance of subsection (2) above to determine an appeal as it applies to a statutory inquiry held by the Secretary of State, but as if in section 12(1) of that Act (statement of reasons for decisions) the reference to any decision taken by the Secretary of State included a reference to a decision taken on his behalf by that person.

(5) A person who determines an appeal under this section on behalf of the Secretary of State and the Secretary of State, if he determines such an appeal, may give such directions as he considers appropriate to give effect to his determination.

(6) The Secretary of State may pay to any person appointed to hear or determine an appeal under this section on his behalf such remuneration and allowances as the Secretary of State may with the approval of the Minister for the Civil Service determine.

(7) In this section—

(a) " licence " means a licence under any of the relevant statutory provisions other than an agricultural licence or nuclear site licence ;

(b) " nuclear site licence " means a licence to use a site for the purpose of installing or operating a nuclear installation within the meaning of the following subsection.

(8) For the purposes of the preceding subsection "nuclear installation " means—

(a) a nuclear reactor (other than such a reactor comprised in a means of transport, whether by land, water or air); or

(b) any other installation of such class or description as may be prescribed for the purposes of this paragraph or section 1(1)(b) of the Nuclear Installations Act 1965, being an installation designed or adapted for—

(i) the production or use of atomic energy ; or

(ii) the carrying out of any process which is preparatory or ancillary to the production or use of atomic energy and which involves or is capable of causing the emission of ionising radiations; or

(iii) the storage, processing or disposal of nuclear fuel or of bulk quantities of other radioactive matter, being matter which has been produced or irradiated in the course of the production or use of nuclear fuel;

and in this subsection—

" atomic energy " has the meaning assigned by the Atomic Energy Act 1946 ;

" nuclear reactor " means any plant (including any machinery, equipment or appliance, whether affixed to land or not) designed or adapted for the production of atomic energy by a fission process in which a controlled chain reaction can be maintained without an additional source of neutrons.

45 Default powers

(1) Where, in the case of a local authority who are an enforcing authority, the Commission is of the opinion that an investigation should be made as to whether that local authority

have failed to perform any of their enforcement functions, the Commission may make a report to the Secretary of State.

(2) The Secretary of State may, after considering a report submitted to him under the preceding subsection, cause a local inquiry to be held; and the provisions of subsections (2) to (5) of section 250 of the Local Government Act 1972 as to local inquiries shall, without prejudice to the generality of subsection (1) of that section, apply to a local inquiry so held as they apply to a local inquiry held in pursuance of that section.

(3) If the Secretary of State is satisfied, after having caused a local inquiry to be held into the matter, that a local authority have failed to perform any of their enforcement functions, he may make an order declaring the authority to be in default.

(4) An order made by virtue of the preceding subsection which declares an authority to be in default may, for the purpose of remedying the default, direct the authority (hereafter in this section referred to as " the defaulting authority ") to perform such of their enforcement functions as are specified in the order in such manner as may be so specified and may specify the time or times within which those functions are to be performed by the authority.

(5) If the defaulting authority fail to comply with any direction contained in such an order the Secretary of State may, instead of enforcing the order by mandamus, make an order transferring to the Executive such of the enforcement functions of the defaulting authority as he thinks fit.

(6) Where any enforcement functions of the defaulting authority are transferred in pursuance of the preceding subsection, the amount of any expenses which the Executive certifies were incurred by it in performing those functions shall on demand be paid to it by the defaulting authority.

(7) Any expenses which in pursuance of the preceding subsection are required to be paid by the defaulting authority in respect of any enforcement functions transferred in pursuance of this section shall be defrayed by the authority in the like manner, and shall be debited to the like account, as if the enforcement functions had not been transferred and the expenses had been incurred by the authority in performing them.

(8) Where the defaulting authority are required to defray any such expenses the authority shall have the like powers for the purpose of raising the money for defraying those expenses as they would have had for the purpose of raising money required for defraying expenses incurred for the purpose of the enforcement functions in question.

(9) An order transferring any enforcement functions of the defaulting authority in pursuance of subsection (5) above may provide for the transfer to the Executive of such of the rights, liabilities and obligations of the authority as the Secretary of State considers appropriate ; and where such an order is revoked the Secretary of State may, by the revoking order or a subsequent order, make such provision as he considers appropriate with respect to any rights, liabilities and obligations held by the Executive for the purposes of the transferred enforcement functions.

(10) The Secretary of State may by order vary or revoke any order previously made by him in pursuance of this section.

(11) In this section "enforcement functions", in relation to a local authority, means the functions of the authority as an enforcing authority.

(12) In the application of this section to Scotland—

(a) in subsection (2) for the words " subsections (2) to (5) of section 250 of the Local Government Act 1972 " there shall be substituted the words " subsections (2) to (8) of section 210 of the Local Government (Scotland) Act 1973 ", except that before 16th May 1975 for the said words there shall be substituted the words " subsections (2) to (9) of section 355 of the Local Government (Scotland) Act 1947 ";

(b) in subsection (5) the words "instead of enforcing the order by mandamus " shall be omitted.

46 Service of notices

(1) Any notice required or authorised by any of the relevant statutory provisions to be served on or given to an inspector may be served or given by delivering it to him or by leaving it at, or sending it by post to, his office.

(2) Any such notice required or authorised to be served on or given to a person other than an inspector may be served or given by delivering it to him, or by leaving it at his proper address, or by sending it by post to him at that address.

(3) Any such notice may—

(a) in the case of a body corporate, be served on or given to the secretary or clerk of that body;

(b) in the case of a partnership, be served on or given to a partner or a person having the control or management of the partnership business or, in Scotland, the firm.

(4) For the purposes of this section and of section 26 of the Interpretation Act 1889 (service of documents by post) in its application to this section, the proper address of any person on or to whom any such notice is to be served or given shall be his last known address, except that—

(a) in the case of a body corporate or their secretary or clerk, it shall be the address of the registered or principal office of that body;

(b) in the case of a partnership or a person having the control or the management of the partnership business, it shall be the principal office of the partnership;

and for the purposes of this subsection the principal office of a company registered outside the United Kingdom or of a partnership carrying on business outside the United Kingdom shall be their principal office within the United Kingdom.

(5) If the person to be served with or given any such notice has specified an address within the United Kingdom other than his proper address within the meaning of subsection (4) above as the one at which he or someone on his behalf will accept notices of the same description as that notice, that address shall also be treated for the purposes of this section and section 26 of the Interpretation Act 1889 as his proper address.

(6) Without prejudice to any other provision of this section, any such notice required or authorised to be served on or given to the owner or occupier of any premises (whether a body corporate or not) may be served or given by sending it by post to him at those premises, or by addressing it by name to the person on or to whom it is to be served or given and delivering it to some responsible person who is or appears to be resident or employed in the premises.

(7) If the name or the address of any owner or occupier of premises on or to whom any such notice as aforesaid is to be served or given cannot after reasonable inquiry be ascertained, the notice may be served or given by addressing it to the person on or to whom it is to be served or given by the description of " owner" or " occupier" of the premises (describing them) to which the notice relates, and by delivering it to some responsible person who is or appears to be resident or employed in the premises, or, if there is no such person to whom it can be delivered, by affixing it or a copy of it to some conspicuous part of the premises.

(8) The preceding provisions of this section shall apply to the sending or giving of a document as they apply to the giving of a notice.

47 Civil liability

(1) Nothing in this Part shall be construed—

- (a) as conferring a right of action in any civil proceedings in respect of any failure to comply with any duty imposed by sections 2 to 7 or any contravention of section 8; or
- (b) as affecting the extent (if any) to which breach of a duty imposed by any of the existing statutory provisions is actionable; or
- (c) as affecting the operation of section 12 of the Nuclear Installations Act 1965 (right to compensation by virtue of certain provisions of that Act).

(2) Breach of a duty imposed by health and safety regulations or agricultural health and safety regulations shall, so far as it causes damage, be actionable except in so far as the regulations provide otherwise.

(3) No provision made by virtue of section 15(6)(b) shall afford a defence in any civil proceedings, whether brought by virtue of subsection (2) above or not; but as regards any duty imposed as mentioned in subsection (2) above health and safety regulations or, as the case may be, agricultural health and safety regulations may provide for any defence specified in the regulations to be available in any action for breach of that duty.

(4) Subsections (1)(a) and (2) above are without prejudice to any right of action which exists apart from the provisions of this Act, and subsection (3) above is without prejudice to any defence which may be available apart from the provisions of the regulations there mentioned.

(5) Any term of an agreement which purports to exclude or restrict the operation of subsection (2) above, or any liability arising by virtue of that subsection shall be void, except in so far as health and safety regulations or, as the case may be, agricultural health and safety regulations provide otherwise.

(6) In this section " damage" includes the death of, or injury to, any person (including any disease and any impairment of a person's physical or mental condition).

48 Application to Crown

(1) Subject to the provisions of this section, the provisions of this Part, except sections 21 to 25 and 33 to 42, and of regulations made under this Part shall bind the Crown.

(2) Although they do not bind the Crown, sections 33 to 42 shall apply to persons in the public service of the Crown as they apply to other persons.

(3) For the purposes of this Part and regulations made thereunder persons in the service of the Crown shall be treated as employees of the Crown whether or not they would be so treated apart from this subsection.

(4) Without prejudice to section 15(5), the Secretary of State may, to the extent that it appears to him requisite or expedient to do so in the interests of the safety of the State or the safe custody of persons lawfully detained, by order exempt the Crown either generally or in particular respects from all or any of the provisions of this Part which would, by virtue of subsection (1) above, bind the Crown.

(5) The power to make orders under this section shall be exercisable by statutory instrument, and any such order may be varied or revoked by a subsequent order.

(6) Nothing in this section shall authorise proceedings to be brought against Her Majesty in her private capacity, and this subsection shall be construed as if section 38(3) of the Crown Proceedings Act 1947 (interpretation of references in that Act to Her Majesty in her private capacity) were contained in this Act.

49 Adaptation of enactments to metric units or appropriate metric units

(1) The appropriate Minister may by regulations amend—

(a) any of the relevant statutory provisions ; or

(b) any provision of an enactment which relates to any matter relevant to any of the general purposes of this Part but is not among the relevant statutory provisions ; or

(c) any provision of an instrument made or having effect under any such enactment as is mentioned in the preceding paragraph,

by substituting an amount or quantity expressed in metric units for an amount or quantity not so expressed or by substituting an amount or quantity expressed in metric units of a description specified in the regulations for an amount or quantity expressed in metric units of a different description.

(2) The amendments shall be such as to preserve the effect of the provisions mentioned except to such extent as in the opinion of the appropriate Minister is necessary to obtain amounts expressed in convenient and suitable terms.

(3) Regulations made by the appropriate Minister under this subsection may, in the case of a provision which falls within any of paragraphs (a) to (c) of subsection (1) above and contains words which refer to units other than metric units, repeal those words if the appropriate Minister is of the opinion that those words could be omitted without altering the effect of that provision.

(4) In this section the appropriate Minister means—

(a) in relation to any provision not relating exclusively to agricultural operations the Secretary of State ;

(b) in relation to any provision relating exclusively to the relevant agricultural purposes that applies to Great Britain or the United Kingdom the Agriculture Ministers;

(c) in relation to any provision so relating that applies to England and Wales only, the Minister of Agriculture, Fisheries and Food;

(d) in relation to any provision so relating that applies to Scotland only, the Secretary of State.

50 Regulations under relevant statutory provisions

(1) Subject to subsection (5) below any power to make regulations conferred on the Secretary of State by any of the relevant statutory provisions may be exercised by him either so as to give effect (with or without modifications) to proposals for the making of regulations by him under that power submitted to him by the Commission or independently of any such proposals, but before making any regulations under any of those provisions independently of any such proposals the Secretary of State shall consult the Commission and such other bodies as appear to him to be appropriate.

(2) Where the Secretary of State proposes to exercise any such power as is mentioned in the preceding subsection so as to give effect to any such proposals as are there mentioned with modifications, he shall, before making the regulations, consult the Commission.

(3) Where the Commission proposes to submit to the Secretary of State any such proposals as are mentioned in subsection (1) above except proposals for the making of regulations under section 43(2), it shall, before so submitting them, consult—

- (a) any government department or other body that appears to the Commission to be appropriate (and, in particular, in the case of proposals for the making of regulations under section 18(2), any body representing local authorities that so appears, and, in the case of proposals for the making of regulations relating to electro-magnetic radiations, the National Radiological Protection Board);
- (b) such government departments and other bodies, if any, as, in relation to any matter dealt with in the proposals, the Commission is required to consult under this subsection by virtue of directions given to it by the Secretary of State.

(4) Where the Minister of Agriculture, Fisheries and Food and the Secretary of State or either of them propose or proposes to make any regulations under any of the relevant statutory provisions, they or he shall before making the regulations consult the Commission and such other bodies as appear to them or him to be appropriate.

(5) Subsections (1) to (3) above shall not apply to any power of the Secretary of State to make regulations which is capable of being exercised by him for Great Britain jointly with the Minister of Agriculture, Fisheries and Food.

51 Exclusion of application to domestic employment

Nothing in this Part shall apply in relation to a person by reason only that he employs another, or is himself employed, as a domestic servant in a private household.

52 Meaning of work and at work

(1) For the purposes of this Part—

- (a) " work" means work as an employee or as a self-employed person;
- (b) an employee is at work throughout the time when he is in the course of his employment, but not otherwise ; and
- (c) a self-employed person is at work throughout such time as he devotes to work as a self-employed person;

and, subject to the following subsection, the expressions " work " and " at work", in whatever context, shall be construed accordingly.

(2) Regulations made under this subsection may—

(a) extend the meaning of " work " and " at work " for the purposes of this Part; and

(b) in that connection provide for any of the relevant statutory provisions to have effect subject to such adaptations as may be specified in the regulations.

(3) The power to make regulations under subsection (2) above shall be exercisable—

(a) in relation to activities not relating exclusively to agricultural operations, by the Secretary of State;

(b) in relation to activities relating exclusively to the relevant agricultural purposes, by the appropriate agriculture authority.

(4) Regulations under subsection (2) above in relation to activities falling within subsection (3)(b) above may be either regulations applying to Great Britain and made by the Minister of Agriculture, Fisheries and Food and the Secretary of State acting jointly, or regulations applying to England and Wales only and made by the said Minister, or regulations applying to Scotland only and made by the Secretary of State; and in subsection (3)(b) above " the appropriate agriculture authority " shall be construed accordingly.

53 General interpretation of Part I

(1) In this Part, unless the context otherwise requires—

" agriculture ", subject to subsection (3) below, includes horticulture, fruit growing, seed growing, dairy farming, livestock breeding and keeping (including the management of livestock up to the point of slaughter or export from Great Britain), forestry, the use of land as grazing land, meadow land, osier land, market gardens and nursery grounds, and the preparation of land for agricultural use, and " agricultural " shall be construed accordingly;

" the Agriculture Ministers " means the Minister of Agriculture, Fisheries and Food and the Secretary of State and, in the case of anything falling to be done by the Agriculture Ministers, means those Ministers acting jointly;

" agricultural health and safety regulations " has the meaning assigned by section 30(1);

" agricultural licence " means a licence of the Agriculture Ministers or either of them under any of the relevant statutory provisions;

" agricultural operation " does not include an agricultural operation performed otherwise than in the course of a trade, business or other undertaking (whether carried on for profit or not) but, subject to subsection (2) below, includes any operation incidental to agriculture which is performed in the course of such a trade, business or undertaking;

" the appropriate Agriculture Minister " means, for the purpose of the application of any of the relevant statutory provisions to England and Wales, the Minister of Agriculture, Fisheries and Food, and, for the purpose of the application of any of those provisions to Scotland, the Secretary of State ;

" article for use at work " means—

(a) any plant designed for use or operation (whether exclusively or not) by persons at work, and

(b) any article designed for use as a component in any such plant;

" code of practice" (without prejudice to section 16(8)) includes a standard, a specification and any other documentary form of practical guidance;

" the Commission " has the meaning assigned by section 10(2);

" conditional sale agreement " means an agreement for the sale of goods under which the purchase price or part of it is payable by instalments, and the property in the goods is to remain in the seller (notwithstanding that the buyer is to be in possession of the goods) until such conditions as to the payment of instalments or otherwise as may be specified in the agreement are fulfilled;

" contract of employment " means a contract of employment or apprenticeship (whether express or implied and, if express, whether oral or in writing);

" credit-sale agreement " means an agreement for the sale of goods, under which the purchase price or part of it is payable by instalments, but which is not a conditional sale agreement;

" domestic premises " means premises occupied as a private dwelling (including any garden, yard, garage, outhouse or other appurtenance of such premises which is not used in common by the occupants of more than one such dwelling), and " non-domestic premises " shall be construed accordingly;

" employee" means an individual who works under a contract of employment, and related expressions shall be construed accordingly;

" enforcing authority " has the meaning assigned by section 18(7);

" the Executive " has the meaning assigned by section 10(5);

" the existing statutory provisions " means the following provisions while and to the extent that they remain in force, namely the provisions of the Acts mentioned in Schedule 1 which are specified in the third column of that Schedule and of the regulations, orders or other instruments of a legislative character made or having effect under any provision so specified ;

" forestry " includes—

(a) the felling of trees and the extraction and primary conversion of trees within the wood or forest in which they were grown, and

(b) the use of land for woodlands where that use is ancillary to the use of land for other agricultural purposes;

" the general purposes of this Part " has the meaning assigned by section 1;

" health and safety regulations " has the meaning assigned by section 15(1);

" hire-purchase agreement " means an agreement other than a conditional sale agreement, under which—

(a) goods are bailed or (in Scotland) hired in return for periodical payments by the person to whom they are bailed or hired ; and

(b) the property in the goods will pass to that person if the terms of the agreement are complied with and one or more of the following occurs:

  (i) the exercise of an option to purchase by that person;

  (ii) the doing of any other specified act by any party to the agreement;

  (iii) the happening of any other event; and " hire-purchase " shall be construed accordingly ;

" improvement notice " means a notice under section 21;

" inspector " means an inspector appointed under section 19;

" livestock " includes any creature kept for the production of food, wool, skins or fur, or for the purpose of its use in the carrying on of any agricultural activity;

" local authority " means—

(a) in relation to England and Wales, a county council, the Greater London Council, a district council, a London borough council, the Common Council of the City of London, the Sub-Treasurer of the Inner Temple or the Under-Treasurer of the Middle Temple,

(b) in relation to Scotland, a regional, islands or district council except that before 16th May 1975 it means a town council or county council;

" offshore installation " means any installation which is intended for underwater exploitation of mineral resources or exploration with a view to such exploitation ;

" personal injury " includes any disease and any impairment of a person's physical or mental condition;

" plant " includes any machinery, equipment or appliance ;

" premises " includes any place and, in particular, includes—

(a) any vehicle, vessel, aircraft or hovercraft,

(b) any installation on land (including the foreshore and other land intermittently covered by water), any offshore installation, and any other installation (whether floating, or resting on the seabed or the subsoil thereof, or resting on other land covered with water or the subsoil thereof), and

(c) any tent or movable structure ;

" prescribed " means prescribed by regulations made by the Secretary of State;

" prohibition notice " means a notice under section 22 ;

" the relevant agricultural purposes " means the following purposes, that is to say—

(a) securing the health, safety and welfare at work of persons engaged in agricultural operations,

(b) protecting persons other than persons so engaged against risks to health or safety arising out of or in connection with the activities at work of persons so engaged; and the reference in paragraph (b) above to the risks there mentioned shall be construed in accordance with section 1(3);

" the relevant statutory provisions " means—

(a) the provisions of this Part and of any health and safety regulations and agricultural health and safety regulations; and

(b) the existing statutory provisions ;

" self-employed person " means an individual who works for gain or reward otherwise than under a contract of employment, whether or not he himself employs others;

" substance " means any natural or artificial substance, whether in solid or liquid form or in the form of a gas or vapour;

" substance for use at work " means any substance intended for use (whether exclusively or not) by persons at work;

" supply ", where the reference is to supplying articles or substances, means supplying them by way of sale, lease, hire or hire-purchase, whether as principal or agent for another.

(2) In determining in any particular case whether an operation is incidental to agriculture within the meaning of the definition of " agricultural operation" in the preceding subsection, regard shall be had to the magnitude of the operation and to the scale on which it is performed as well as to all other relevant circumstances.

(3) Provision may be made by order for directing that for the purposes of this Part any activity or operation specified in the order which would or would not otherwise be agriculture within the meaning of this Part shall be treated as not being or, as the case may be, being agriculture for those purposes.

(4) An order under subsection (3) above may be either an order applying to Great Britain and made by the Minister of Agriculture, Fisheries and Food and the Secretary of State acting jointly, or an order applying to England and Wales only and made by the said Minister, or an order applying to Scotland only and made by the Secretary of State.

(5) An order under subsection (3) above may be varied or revoked by a subsequent order thereunder made by the authority who made the original order.

(6) The power to make orders under subsection (3) above shall be exercisable by statutory instrument subject to annulment in pursuance of a resolution of either House of Parliament.

54 Application of Part I to Isles of Scilly

This Part, in its application to the Isles of Stilly, shall apply as if those Isles were a local government area and the Council of those Isles were a local authority.

PART II

THE EMPLOYMENT MEDICAL ADVISORY SERVICE

55 Functions of, and responsibility for maintaining, employment medical advisory service

(1) There shall continue to be an employment medical advisory service, which shall be maintained for the following purposes, that is to say—
- (a) securing that the Secretary of State, the Health and Safety Commission, the Manpower Services Commission and others concerned with the health of employed persons or of persons seeking or training for employment can be kept informed of, and adequately advised on, matters of which they ought respectively to take cognisance concerning the safeguarding and improvement of the health of those persons;
- (b) giving to employed persons and persons seeking or training for employment information and advice on health in relation to employment and training for employment;
- (c) other purposes of the Secretary of State's functions relating to employment.

(2) The authority responsible for maintaining the said service shall be the Secretary of State; but if arrangements are made by the Secretary of State for that responsibility to be discharged on his behalf by the Health and Safety Commission or some other body, then, while those arrangements operate, the body so discharging that responsibility (and not the Secretary of State) shall be the authority responsible for maintaining that service.

(3) The authority for the time being responsible for maintaining the said service may also for the purposes mentioned in subsection (1) above, and for the purpose of assisting employment medical advisers in the performance of their functions, investigate or

assist in, arrange for or make payments in respect of the investigation of problems arising in connection with any such matters as are so mentioned or otherwise in connection with the functions of employment medical advisers, and for the purpose of investigating or assisting in the investigation of such problems may provide and maintain such laboratories and other services as appear to the authority to be requisite.

(4) Any arrangements made by the Secretary of State in pursuance of subsection (2) above may be terminated by him at any time, but without prejudice to the making of other arrangements at any time in pursuance of that subsection (including arrangements which are to operate from the time when any previous arrangements so made cease to operate).

(5) Without prejudice to sections 11(4)(a) and 12(b), it shall be the duty of the Health and Safety Commission, if so directed by the Secretary of State, to enter into arrangements with him for the Commission to be responsible for maintaining the said service.

(6) In subsection (1) above—

(a) the reference to persons training for employment shall include persons attending industrial rehabilitation courses provided by virtue of the Employment and Training Act 1973 ; and

(b) the reference to persons (other than the Secretary of State and the Commissions there mentioned) concerned with the health of employed persons or of persons seeking or training for employment shall be taken to include organisations representing employers, employees and occupational health practitioners respectively.

56 Functions of authority responsible for maintaining the service

(1) The authority for the time being responsible for maintaining the employment medical advisory service shall for the purpose of discharging that responsibility appoint persons to be employment medical advisers, and may for that purpose appoint such other officers and servants as it may determine, subject however to the requisite approval as to numbers, that is to say—

(a) where that authority is the Secretary of State, the approval of the Minister for the Civil Service;

(b) otherwise, the approval of the Secretary of State given with the consent of that Minister.

(2) A person shall not be qualified to be appointed, or to be, an employment medical adviser unless he is a fully registered medical practitioner.

(3) The authority for the time being responsible for maintaining the said service may determine the cases and circumstances in which the employment medical advisers or any of them are to perform the duties or exercise the powers conferred on employment medical advisers by or under this Act or otherwise.

(4) Where as a result of arrangements made in pursuance of section 55(2) the authority responsible for maintaining the said service changes, the change shall not invalidate any appointment previously made under subsection (1) above, and any such appointment subsisting when the change occurs shall thereafter have effect as if made by the new authority.

57 Fees

(1) The Secretary of State may by regulations provide for such fees as may be fixed by or determined under the regulations to be payable for or in connection with the performance by the authority responsible for maintaining the employment medical advisory service of any function conferred for the purposes of that service on that authority by virtue of this Part or otherwise.

(2) For the purposes of this section, the performance by an employment medical adviser of his functions shall be treated as the performance by the authority responsible for maintaining the said service of functions conferred on that authority as mentioned in the preceding subsection.

(3) The provisions of subsections (4), (5) and (8) of section 43 shall apply in relation to regulations under this section with the modification that references to subsection (2) of that section shall be read as references to subsection (1) of this section.

(4) Where an authority other than the Secretary of State is responsible for maintaining the said service, the Secretary of State shall consult that authority before making any regulations under this section.

58 Other financial provisions

(1) The authority for the time being responsible for maintaining the employment medical advisory service may pay—

- (a) to employment medical advisers such salaries or such fees and travelling or other allowances; and
- (b) to other persons called upon to give advice in connection with the execution of the authority's functions under this Part such travelling or other allowances or compensation for loss of remunerative time; and
- (c) to persons attending for medical examinations conducted by, or in accordance with arrangements made by, employment medical advisers (including pathological, physiological and radiological tests and similar investigations so conducted) such travelling or subsistence allowances or such compensation for loss of earnings,

as the authority may, with the requisite approval, determine.

(2) For the purposes of the preceding subsection the requisite approval is—

- (a) where the said authority is the Secretary of State, the approval of the Minister for the Civil Service ;
- (b) otherwise, the approval of the Secretary of State given with the consent of that Minister.

(3) Where an authority other than the Secretary of State is responsible for maintaining the said service, it shall be the duty of the Secretary of State to pay to that authority such sums as are approved by the Treasury and as he considers appropriate for the purpose of enabling the authority to discharge that responsibility.

59 Duty of responsible authority to keep accounts and to report

(1) It shall be the duty of the authority for the time being responsible for maintaining the employment medical advisory service—

(a) to keep, in relation to the maintenance of that service, proper accounts and proper records in relation to the accounts;

(b) to prepare in respect of each accounting year a statement of accounts relating to the maintenance of that service in such form as the Secretary of State may direct with the approval of the Treasury; and

(c) to send copies of the statement to the Secretary of State and the Comptroller and Auditor General before the end of the month of November next following the accounting year to which the statement relates.

(2) The Comptroller and Auditor General shall examine, certify and report on each statement received by him in pursuance of subsection (1) above and shall lay copies of each statement and of his report before each House of Parliament.

(3) It shall also be the duty of the authority responsible for maintaining the employment medical advisory service to make to the Secretary of State, as soon as possible after the end of each accounting year, a report on the discharge of its responsibilities in relation to that service during that year; and the Secretary of State shall lay before each House of Parliament a copy of each report made to him in pursuance of this subsection.

(4) Where as a result of arrangements made in pursuance of section 55(2) the authority responsible for maintaining the employment medical advisory service changes, the change shall not affect any duty imposed by this section on the body which was responsible for maintaining that service before the change.

(5) No duty imposed on the authority for the time being responsible for maintaining the employment medical advisory service by subsection (1) or (3) above shall fall on the Commission (which is subject to corresponding duties under Schedule 2) or on the Secretary of State.

(6) In this section " accounting year " means, except so far as the Secretary of State otherwise directs, the period of twelve months ending with 31st March in any year.

60 Supplementary

(1) It shall be the duty of the Secretary of State to secure that each Area Health Authority arranges for one of its officers who is a fully registered medical practitioner to furnish, on the application of an employment medical adviser, such particulars of the school medical record of a person who has not attained the age of eighteen and such other information relating to his medical history as the adviser may reasonably require for the efficient performance of his functions; but no particulars or information about any person which may be furnished to an adviser in pursuance of this subsection shall (without the consent of that person) be disclosed by the adviser otherwise than for the efficient performance of his functions.

(2) In its application to Scotland the preceding subsection shall have effect with the substitution of the words " every Health Board arrange for one of their " for the words from " each " to " its ".

(3) The Secretary of State may by order made by statutory instrument subject to annulment in pursuance of a resolution of either House of Parliament modify the provisions of section 7(3) and (4) of the Employment and Training Act 1973 (which require a person's period of continuous employment by a relevant body or in the civil service of the State to be treated, for the purposes of sections 1 and 2 of the Contracts of Employment Act 1972 and of certain provisions of the Industrial Relations Act

1971 affecting the right of an employee not to be unfairly dismissed, as increased by reference to previous periods of continuous employment by such a body or in that service) for the purpose of securing that employment as an employment medical adviser by an authority other than the Secretary of State is similarly treated for those purposes.

An order under this subsection may be varied or revoked by a subsequent order thereunder.

(4) References to the chief employment medical adviser or a deputy chief employment medical adviser in any provision of an enactment or instrument made under an enactment shall be read as references to a person appointed for the purposes of that provision by the authority responsible for maintaining the employment medical advisory service.

(5) The following provisions of the Employment Medical Advisory Service Act 1972 (which are superseded by the preceding provisions of this Part or rendered unnecessary by provisions contained in Part I), namely sections 1 and 6 and Schedule 1, shall cease to have effect; but—

(a) in so far as anything done under or by virtue of the said section 1 or Schedule 1 could have been done under or by virtue of a corresponding provision of Part I or this Part, it shall not be invalidated by the repeal of that section and Schedule by this Act but shall have effect as if done under or by virtue of that corresponding provision; and

(b) any order made under the said section 6 which is in force immediately before the repeal of that section by this Act shall remain in force notwithstanding that repeal, but may be revoked or varied by regulations under section 43(2) or 57, as if it were an instrument containing regulations made under section 43(2) or 57, as the case may require.

(6) Where any Act (whether passed before, or in the same Session as, this Act) or any document refers, either expressly or by implication, to or to any enactment contained in any of the provisions of the said Act of 1972 which are mentioned in the preceding subsection, the reference shall, except where the context otherwise requires, be construed as, or as including, a reference to the corresponding provision of this Act.

(7) Nothing in subsection (5) or (6) above shall be taken as prejudicing the operation of section 38 of the Interpretation Act 1889 (which relates to the effect of repeals).

PART III

BUILDING REGULATIONS, AND AMENDMENT OF BUILDING (SCOTLAND) ACT 1959

61 Amendments of enactments relating to building regulations

(1) For sections 61 and 62 of the 1936 Act (power to make building regulations, and their application to existing buildings) there shall be substituted the following sections—

"61 Power to make building regulations

(1) Subject to the provisions of Part II of the Public Health Act 1961, the Secretary of State shall have power, for any of the purposes mentioned in subsection (2) below, to make regulations with respect to the design and

construction of buildings and the provision of services, fittings and equipment in or in connection with buildings. Regulations under this subsection shall be known as building regulations.

(2) The purposes referred to in the preceding subsection are the following, that is to say—

(a) securing the health, safety, welfare and convenience of persons in or about buildings and of others who may be affected by buildings or matters connected with buildings;

(b) furthering the conservation of fuel and power; and

(c) preventing waste, undue consumption, misuse or contamination of water.

(3) Building regulations may—

(a) provide for particular requirements of the regulations to be deemed to be complied with where prescribed methods of construction, prescribed types of materials or other prescribed means are used in or in connection with buildings;

(b) be framed to any extent by reference to a document published by or on behalf of the Secretary of State or any other person or any body, or by reference to the approval or satisfaction of any prescribed person or body.

(4) Building regulations may include provision as to—

(a) the giving of notices ;

(b) the deposit of plans of proposed work or work already executed (including provision as to the number of copies to be deposited);

(c) the retention by local authorities of copies of plans deposited with them in accordance with the regulations;

(d) the inspection and testing of work;

(e) the taking of samples.

(5) Building regulations may exempt from all or any of the provisions of building regulations any prescribed class of buildings, services, fittings or equipment.

(6) The Secretary of State may by direction exempt from all or any of the provisions of building regulations any particular building or, as regards any particular location, buildings of any particular class thereat, and may in either case do so either unconditionally or subject to compliance with any conditions specified in the direction.

(7) A person who contravenes any condition specified in a direction given under the preceding subsection or permits any such condition to be contravened shall be liable to a fine not exceeding £400 and to a further fine not exceeding £50 for each day on which the offence continues after he is convicted.

(8) For the purposes of building regulations and of any direction given or instrument made with reference to building regulations, buildings may be classified by reference to size, description, design, purpose, location or any other characteristic whatsoever.

62 Application of building regulations to existing buildings etc.

(1) Building regulations may be made with respect to—

(a) alterations and extensions of buildings and of services, fittings and equipment in or in connection with buildings;

(b) new services, fittings, or equipment provided in or in connection with buildings;

(c) buildings and services, fittings and equipment in or in connection with buildings, so far as affected by—

(i) alterations or extensions of buildings ; or

(ii) new, altered or extended services, fittings or equipment in or in connection with buildings;

(d) the whole of any building, together with any services, fittings or equipment provided in or in connection therewith, in respect of which there are or are proposed to be carried out any operations which by virtue of section 74(1)(c) of the Health and Safety at Work etc. Act 1974 constitute the construction of a building for the purposes of this section ;

(e) buildings or parts of buildings, together with any services, fittings or equipment provided in or in connection therewith, in cases where the purposes for which or the manner or circumstances in which a building or part of a building is used change or changes in a way that constitutes a material change of use of the building or part within the meaning of the expression ' material change of use' as defined for the purposes of this paragraph by building regulations.

(2) So far as they relate to matters mentioned in the preceding subsection, building regulations may be made to apply to or in connection with buildings erected before the date on which the regulations came into force but, except as aforesaid (and subject to section 65(2) of the Health and Safety at Work etc. Act 1974) shall not apply to buildings erected before that date.".

(2) Without prejudice to the generality of subsection (1) of section 61 of the 1936 Act as substituted by this section, building regulations may for any of the purposes mentioned in subsection (2) of that section make provision with respect to any of the matters mentioned in Schedule 5, may require things to be provided or done in or in connection with buildings (as well as regulating the provision or doing of things in or in connection with buildings), and may prescribe the manner in which work is to be carried out.

(3) The enactments relating to building regulations shall have effect subject to the further amendments provided for in Part I of Schedule 6.

(4) Section 65 of the 1936 Act and sections 4, 6 and 7 of the 1961 Act, as they will have effect after the coming into force of the preceding subsection, are set out in Part II of the said Schedule 6.

(5) Section 71 of the 1936 Act (exemption of certain buildings from building regulations) shall cease to have effect.

(6) Any regulations under section 4 of the 1961 Act which are in force immediately before the repeal of subsection (1) of that section by this Act shall not be invalidated by

that repeal, but shall have effect as if made under section 61(1) of the 1936 Act as substituted by this section.

62 Further matters for which building regulations may provide

(1) Building regulations may make provision for requiring local authorities in such circumstances as may be prescribed to consult any prescribed person before taking any prescribed step in connection with any work or other matter to which building regulations are applicable.

(2) Building regulations—

(a) may authorise local authorities to accept, as evidence that the requirements of building regulations as to matters of any prescribed description are or would be satisfied, certificates to that effect by persons of any class or description prescribed in relation to those matters or by a person nominated in writing by the Secretary of State in any particular case ;

(b) may provide for the issue by local authorities of certificates to the effect that, so far as the authority concerned have been able to ascertain after taking all reasonable steps in that behalf, the requirements of building regulations as to matters of any prescribed description are satisfied in any particular case, and for such certificates to be evidence (but not conclusive evidence) of compliance with the regulations ;

(c) may make provision—

(i) for prohibiting, in prescribed circumstances, the carrying out of proposed work of any prescribed class involving matters of any prescribed description unless there has been deposited with the prescribed authority as regards those matters a certificate such as is mentioned in paragraph (a) above ;

(ii) for enabling, in cases where such a certificate is required by virtue of the preceding sub-paragraph, any dispute as to whether a certificate ought to be issued to be referred to the Secretary of State; and

(iii) for enabling the Secretary of State, on any such reference, to give such directions as he thinks fit.

(3) Building regulations may authorise local authorities to charge prescribed fees for or in connection with the performance of prescribed functions of theirs relating to building regulations.

(4) Building regulations may make a prescribed person or class of persons responsible (instead of local authorities) for performing prescribed functions of local authorities under or in connection with building regulations, and for that purpose may provide for any prescribed enactment relating to building regulations and any prescribed provision of such regulations to apply (with any prescribed modifications) in relation to a prescribed person or a person of a prescribed class as that enactment or provision applies in relation to a local authority.

(5) Building regulations may repeal or modify any enactment to which this subsection applies if it appears to the Secretary of State that the enactment is inconsistent with, or is unnecessary or requires alteration in consequence of, any provision contained in or made under any enactment relating to building regulations.

This subsection applies to any enactment contained in this Act or in any other Act passed before or in the same Session as this Act, other than sections 61 to 71 of the 1936 Act, sections 4 to 11 of, and Schedule 1 to, the 1961 Act, and this Part.

63 Miscellaneous provisions as to the approval of plans

(1) A local authority with whom plans of any proposed work are deposited in accordance with building regulations may in prescribed cases pass them by stages in accordance with the regulations and, where a local authority pass any such plans to a limited extent at any stage.—

(a) they shall impose conditions as to the depositing of further plans in connection with the proposed work; and

(b) they may impose conditions for securing that, pending the deposit of such of the further plans as they may indicate, the proposed work will not be proceeded with except to such extent as they may in accordance with the regulations authorise.

(2) A person who contravenes any condition imposed by a local authority under subsection (1) above other than a condition as to the depositing of further plans, or permits any such condition to be contravened, shall be liable to a fine not exceeding £400 and to a further fine not exceeding £50 for each day on which the offence continues after he is convicted.

(3) A local authority with whom plans of any proposed work are deposited in accordance with building regulations may, notwithstanding that the plans are defective or show that the work would contravene any of the building regulations, pass the plans provisionally, that is to say, subject to any modifications which they think necessary for remedying the defect or avoiding the contravention, indicating the modifications in the notice of approval and—

(a) if, within a prescribed time and in a prescribed manner so indicated, the person by or on behalf of whom the plans were deposited notifies the authority that he agrees to the modifications, the plans shall be treated as having been passed subject to those modifications; and

(b) if not, the plans shall be treated as having been rejected.

(4) In cases where by virtue of subsection (1) or (3) above plans are passed by stages or provisionally, the provisions of section 64(1) to (3) of the 1936 Act shall have effect subject to such modifications as may be prescribed.

(5) Where plans of any proposed work have been passed under section 64 of the 1936 Act by a local authority, the person by or on behalf of whom the plans were in accordance with building regulations deposited with the authority may, and in such cases as may be prescribed shall, for the purpose of obtaining the approval of the authority to any proposed departure or deviation from the plans as passed, deposit plans of any such departure or deviation ; and that section shall apply in relation to plans deposited under this subsection as it applies in relation to the plans originally deposited.

(6) Where in accordance with any existing enactment (however framed or worded) plans of a proposed building of any prescribed class are submitted to a Minister of the Crown for his approval—

(a) plans of the proposed building shall not be required to be deposited with the local authority for the purposes of section 64 of the 1936 Act in pursuance of building regulations;

(b) the Minister shall not approve the plans unless he is satisfied that, so far as applicable, the substantive requirements of building regulations will be complied with by and in connection with the proposed building;

(c) the approval of the plans by the Minister shall operate, for such purposes as may be prescribed, in the same way as the passing of them by the local authority would have operated;

(d) the Minister may exercise in connection with the proposed building the like powers of dispensing with or relaxing requirements of building regulations as are conferred on the Secretary of State and local authorities by virtue of section 6 of the 1961 Act (other than a power excepted by subsection (7) below), subject however to the like requirements as to consultation (if any) as apply by virtue of section 62(1) in the case of a local authority (but not to the requirements in the said section 6 as to consultation with the local authority) and to the like requirements as in the case of the Secretary of State apply by virtue of section 8 of the 1961 Act (opportunity to make representations about proposal to relax building regulations).

(7) In the preceding subsection " existing enactment" means an enactment passed before the coming into force of that subsection, other than an enactment relating to town and country planning; and the power excepted from paragraph (d) of that subsection is one which by virtue of section 62(4) is exercisable otherwise than by a local authority.

64 Special provisions as to materials etc. unsuitable for permanent buildings

(1) This section applies—

(a) to any work consisting of a part of a building, being a part in the construction of which there is used any material or component of a type which, in relation to a part of that description, is prescribed for the purposes of this paragraph under subsection (2) below; and

(b) to any work provided in or in connection with a building, being work consisting of a service, fitting or item of equipment of a type so prescribed for the purposes of this paragraph.

(2) The Secretary of State may by building regulations—

(a) prescribe a type of material or component for the purposes of subsection (1)(a) above if in his opinion materials or components of that type are likely to be unsuitable for use in the construction of a particular part of a permanent building in the absence of conditions with respect to the use of the building or with respect to any material or component of that type used in the construction of a part of that description;

(b) prescribe a type of service, fitting or equipment for the purposes of subsection (1)(b) above if in his opinion services, fittings or equipment of that type are likely to be unsuitable for provision in or in connection with a permanent building in the absence of conditions with respect to the use of the building or with respect to any service, fitting or equipment of that type so provided.

(3) Where plans of any proposed work are, in accordance with building regulations, deposited with a local authority and the plans show that the proposed work would include or consist of work to which this section applies, the authority may, notwithstanding that the plans conform with the regulations—

(a) reject the plans ; or

(b) in passing the plans fix a period on the expiration of which the work to which this section applies or the relevant building (as the authority may in passing the plans direct) must be removed and, if they think fit, impose with respect to the use of the relevant building or with respect to the work to which this section applies such reasonable conditions, if any, as they consider appropriate, so however that no condition as to the use of the relevant building shall be imposed which conflicts with any condition imposed or having effect as if imposed under Part III or IV of the Town and Country Planning Act 1971.

(4) If, in the case of any work in respect of which plans ought by virtue of building regulations to have been deposited with a local authority but have not been so deposited, the work appears to the authority to include or consist of work to which this section applies, the authority, without prejudice to their right to take proceedings in respect of any contravention of the regulations, may fix a period on the expiration of which the work to which this section applies or the relevant building (as the authority may in fixing the period direct) must be removed and, if they think fit, impose any conditions that might have been imposed under the preceding subsection in passing plans for the first-mentioned work and, where they fix such a period, shall forthwith give notice thereof, and of any conditions imposed, to the owner of the relevant building.

(5) If, in the case of any work appearing to the local authority to fall within subsection (1) (b) above, plans of the work were not required by building regulations to be deposited with the authority, and were not so deposited, the authority may at any time within twelve months from the date of completion of the work fix a period on the expiration of which the work must be removed and, if they think fit, impose any conditions which, if plans of the work had been required to be, and had been, so deposited, might have been imposed under subsection (3) above in passing the plans and, where they fix such a period, shall forthwith give notice thereof, and of any conditions imposed, to the owner of the relevant building.

(6) A local authority may from time to time extend any period fixed, or vary any conditions imposed, under this section, but so that, unless an application in that behalf is made to them by the owner of the relevant building, they shall not exercise their power of varying conditions so imposed except when granting an extension or further extension of the period fixed with respect to the work or building, as the case may be.

(7) Any person aggrieved by the action of a local authority under this section in rejecting plans, or in fixing or refusing to extend any period, or in imposing or refusing to vary any conditions, may appeal to the Secretary of State within the prescribed time and in the prescribed manner.

(8) Where a period has been fixed under this section with respect to any work to which this section applies or with respect to the relevant building, the owner of that building shall on the expiration of that period or, as the case may be, of that period as extended, remove the work or building with respect to which the period was fixed ; and if he fails to do so, the local authority may remove that work or building, as the case may be, and may recover from him the expenses reasonably incurred by them in doing so.

(9) A person who—

(a) contravenes any condition imposed under this section or permits any such condition to be contravened; or

(b) contravenes subsection (8) above;

shall be liable to a fine not exceeding £400 and to a further fine not exceeding £50 for each day on which the offence continues or, as the case may be, on which the work or building is allowed to remain, after he is convicted; but this subsection shall not be construed as prejudicing a local authority's rights under subsection (8) above.

(10) In this section " the relevant building " means, in any particular case, the building mentioned in paragraph (a) or, as the case may be, paragraph (b) of subsection (1) above

(11) Section 53 of the 1936 Act (which is superseded by the preceding provisions of this section) shall cease to have effect, but—

(a) any building regulations made, period fixed, condition imposed or other thing done by virtue of that section shall be deemed to have been made, fixed, imposed or done by virtue of this section ; and

(b) anything begun under that section may be continued under this Act as if begun under this section, so however that any appeal under subsection (4) of that section which is pending at the time when that section ceases to have effect, and any proceedings arising out of such appeal, shall proceed as if that section were still in force.

65 Continuing requirements

(1) Building regulations may impose on owners and occupiers of buildings to which building regulations are applicable such continuing requirements as the Secretary of State considers appropriate for securing, with respect to any provision of building regulations designated in the regulations as a provision to which those requirements relate, that the purposes of that provision are not frustrated; but a continuing requirement imposed by virtue of this subsection shall not apply in relation to a building unless a provision of building regulations so designated as one to which the requirement relates applies to that building.

(2) Building regulations may impose on owners and occupiers of buildings of any prescribed class (whenever erected, and whether or not any building regulations were applicable to them at the time of their erection) continuing requirements with respect to all or any of the following matters, namely—

(a) the conditions subject to which any services, fittings or equipment provided in or in connection with any building of that class may be used;

(b) the inspection and maintenance of any services, fittings or equipment so provided ; and

(c) the making of reports to any prescribed authority on the condition of any services, fittings or equipment so provided;

and so much of section 62 of the 1936 Act as restricts the application of building regulations shall not apply to regulations made by virtue of this subsection.

(3) If a person contravenes a continuing requirement imposed by virtue of this section, the local authority, without prejudice to their right to take proceedings for a fine in respect of the contravention, may execute any work or take any other action required to remedy the contravention, and may recover from that person the expenses reasonably incurred by them in so doing.

(4) Where a local authority have power under the preceding subsection to execute any work or take any other action they may, instead of exercising that power, by notice

require the owner or the occupier of the building to which the contravention referred to in that subsection relates to execute that work or take that action.

The provisions of Part XII of the 1936 Act with respect to appeals against, and the enforcement of, notices requiring the execution of works shall apply in relation to any notice given under this section, subject however to the modification that in those provisions references to the execution of works shall be construed as references to the execution of work or the taking of other action, and references to work shall be construed accordingly.

(5) The provisions of sections 6, 7 and 8 of the 1961 Act (power to dispense with or relax requirements in building regulations, and related provisions) shall have effect in relation to continuing requirements imposed by virtue of this section subject to the following modifications, that is to say—

(a) a direction under the said section 6 shall, if it so provides, cease to have effect at the end of such period as may be specified in the direction ; and

(b) in subsection (1) of the said section 7 (as amended by this Act), the reference to granting an application subject to conditions shall be read as including a reference to granting an application for a limited period.

66 Type relaxation of building regulations

(1) If the Secretary of State considers that the operation of any requirement of building regulations would be unreasonable in relation to any particular type of building matter, he may, either on an application made to him or of his own accord, give a direction dispensing with or relaxing that requirement generally in relation to that type of building matter, either unconditionally or subject to compliance with any conditions specified in the direction, being conditions with respect to matters directly connected with the dispensation or relaxation.

(2) A direction under subsection (1) above—

(a) shall, if it so provides, cease to have effect at the end of such period as may be specified in the direction;

(b) may be varied or revoked by a subsequent direction of the Secretary of State.

(3) Building regulations may require a person making an application under subsection (1) above to pay the Secretary of State the prescribed fee; and, without prejudice to section 4(2) of the 1961 Act, regulations made by virtue of this subsection may prescribe different fees for different cases:

Provided that the Secretary of State may in any particular case remit the whole or part of any fee payable by virtue of this subsection.

(4) Before giving a direction under this section the Secretary of State shall consult such bodies as appear to him to be representative of the interests concerned (including in particular, in the case of a direction that relates to a requirement relevant to any of their functions, the National Water Council).

(5) Where the Secretary of State gives a direction under this section, he shall publish notice of that fact in such manner as he thinks fit.

(6) A person who contravenes any condition specified in a direction given under this section or permits any such condition to be contravened shall be liable to a fine not exceeding £400 and to a further fine not exceeding £50 for each day on which the offence continues after he is convicted.

(7) If at any time a direction under subsection (1) above dispensing with or relaxing a requirement of building regulations ceases to have effect by virtue of subsection (2)(c) above or is varied or revoked under subsection (2)(b) above, mat fact shall not affect the continued operation of the direction (with any conditions specified therein) in any case in which before that time—

(a) plans of the proposed work were, in accordance with building regulations, deposited with a local authority; or

(b) a building notice was served on the district surveyor in pursuance of section 83 of the London Building Acts (Amendment) Act 1939.

(8) In this section and section 67 below " building matter " means any building or other matter whatsoever to which building regulations are in any circumstances applicable.

67 Power of Secretary of State to approve types of building etc.

(1) The following provisions of this section shall have effect with a view to enabling the Secretary of State, either on an application made to him or of his own accord, to approve any particular type of building matter as complying, either generally or in any class of case, with particular requirements of building regulations.

(2) An application for the approval under this section of a type of building matter shall comply with any requirements of building regulations as to the form of such applications and the particulars to be included therein.

(3) Where under subsection (1) above the Secretary of State approves a type of building matter as complying with particular requirements of building regulations either generally or in any class of case, he may issue a certificate to that effect specifying—

(a) the type of building matter to which the certificate relates ;

(b) the requirements of building regulations to which the certificate relates; and

(c) where applicable, the class or classes of case to which the certificate applies.

(4) A certificate under this section shall, if it so provides, cease to have effect at the end of such period as may be specified in the certificate.

(5) If, while a certificate under this section is in force, it is found, in any particular case involving a building matter of the type to which the certificate relates, that the building matter in question is of that type and the case is one to which the certificate applies, that building matter shall in that particular case be deemed to comply with the requirements of building regulations to which the certificate relates.

(6) The Secretary of State may vary a certificate under this section either on an application made to him or of his own accord; but in the case of a certificate issued on an application made by a person under subsection (1) above, the Secretary of State, except where he varies it on the application of that person, shall before varying it give that person reasonable notice that he proposes to do so.

(7) Building regulations may require a person making an application under subsection (1) or (6) above to pay the Secretary of State the prescribed fee ; and, without prejudice to section 4(2) of the 1961 Act, regulations made by virtue of this subsection may prescribe different fees for different cases:

Provided that the Secretary of State may in any particular case remit the whole or part of any fee payable by virtue of this subsection.

(8) The Secretary of State may revoke a certificate issued under this section, but before doing so in the case of a certificate issued on an application under subsection (1) above shall give the person on whose application the certificate was issued reasonable notice that he proposes to do so.

(9) Where the Secretary of State issues a certificate under this section or varies or revokes a certificate so issued, he shall publish notice of that fact in such manner as he thinks fit.

(10) If at any time a certificate under this section ceases to have effect by virtue of subsection (4) above or is varied or revoked under the preceding provisions of this section, that fact shall not affect the continued operation of subsection (5) above by virtue of that certificate in any case in which before that time—

(a) plans of the proposed work were, in accordance with building regulations, deposited with a local authority; or

(b) a building notice was served on the district surveyor in pursuance of section 83 of the London Building Acts (Amendment) Act 1939.

(11) For the purposes of subsection (3) above or any variation of a certificate under subsection (6) above, a class of case may be framed in any way that the Secretary of State thinks fit.

(12) The Secretary of State may by building regulations delegate to any person or body, to such extent and subject to such conditions as the Secretary of State may think fit, the powers of approval conferred on him by this section; and so far as those powers are for the time being so delegated to any person or body, the preceding provisions of this section, except so much of subsection (7) as precedes the proviso, and any building regulation made by virtue of that subsection shall (subject to any prescribed conditions) have effect in relation to that person or body with the substitution of references to that person or body for references to the Secretary of State.

68 Power to require or carry out tests for conformity with building regulations

(1) The following subsection shall have effect for the purpose of enabling a local authority to ascertain, as regards any work or proposed work to which building regulations for the enforcement of which they are responsible are applicable, whether any provision of building regulations is or would be contravened by, or by anything done or proposed to be done in connection with, that work.

(2) The local authority shall have power for that purpose—

(a) to require any person by whom or on whose behalf the work was, is being or is proposed to be done to carry out such reasonable tests of or in connection with the work as may be specified in the requirement; or

(b) themselves to carry out any reasonable tests of or in connection with the work, and to take any samples necessary to enable them to carry out any such test.

(3) Without prejudice to the generality of the preceding subsection, the matters with respect to which tests may be required or carried out under that subsection include—

(a) tests of the soil or subsoil of the site of any building ;

(b) tests of any material, component or combination of components which has been, is being or is proposed to be used in the construction of a building, and tests of any service, fitting or equipment which has been, is being or is proposed to be provided in or in connection with a building.

(4) A local authority shall have power, for the purpose of ascertaining whether there is or has been, in the case of any building, any contravention of any continuing requirement that applies in relation to that building—

(a) to require the owner or occupier of the building to carry out such reasonable tests as may be specified in the requirement under this paragraph ; or

(b) themselves to carry out any tests which they have power to require under the preceding paragraph, and to take any samples necessary to enable them to carry out any such test. In this subsection " continuing requirement" means a continuing requirement imposed by building regulations made by virtue of section 65(1) or (2).

(5) The expense of carrying out any tests which a person is required to carry out under this section shall be met by that person:

Provided that the local authority, on an application made to them, may, if they think it reasonable to do so, direct that the expense of carrying out any such tests, or such part of that expense as may be specified in the direction, shall be met by the local authority.

(6) Any question arising under this section between a local authority and any person as to the reasonableness—

(a) of any test specified in a requirement imposed on him by the authority under this section ; or

(b) of a refusal by the authority to give a direction under subsection (5) above on an application made by him; or

(c) of a direction under that subsection given on such an application,

may on the application of that person be determined by a court of summary jurisdiction ; and in a case falling within paragraph (b) or (c) above the court may order the expense to which the application relates to be met by the local authority to such extent as the court thinks just.

69 Provisions relating to appeals etc. to the Secretary of State under certain provisions

(1) On an appeal to the Secretary of State under section 64 of the 1936 Act, section 7 of the 1961 Act or section 64 of this Act, the Secretary of State may at his discretion afford to the appellant and the local authority an opportunity of appearing before, and being heard by, a person appointed by the Secretary of State for the purpose.

(2) On determining any such appeal as is mentioned in subsection (1) above, the Secretary of State shall give such directions, if any, as he considers appropriate for giving effect to his determination.

(3) Where the Secretary of State gives a decision in proceedings—

(a) on any such appeal as is mentioned in subsection (1) above; or

(b) on a reference under section 67 of the 1936 Act; or

(c) on any application for a direction under section 6 of the 1961 Act where the power of giving the direction is not exercisable by the local authority,

the relevant person or the local authority may appeal to the High Court against the decision on a point of law.

In this subsection " the relevant person "—

(i) as regards such an appeal as is mentioned in paragraph (a) above, means the appellant;

(ii) as regards a reference under the said section 67, means the person on whose application (jointly with the local authority) the reference was made ;

(iii) as regards any such application as is mentioned in paragraph (c) above, means the applicant.

(4) At any stage of the proceedings on any such appeal, reference or application as is mentioned in the preceding subsection, the Secretary of State may state any question of law arising in the course of the proceedings in the form of a special case for the decision of the High Court; and a decision of the High Court on a case stated by virtue of this subsection shall be deemed to be a judgment of the court within the meaning of section 27 of the Supreme Court of Judicature (Consolidation) Act 1925 (jurisdiction of the Court of Appeal to hear and determine appeals from any judgment of the High Court).

(5) In relation to any proceedings in the High Court or the Court of Appeal brought by virtue of this section the power to make rules of court shall include power to make rules—

(a) prescribing the powers of the High Court or the Court of Appeal with respect to the remitting of the matter with the opinion or direction of the court for re-hearing and determination by the Secretary of State ; and

(b) providing for the Secretary of State, either generally or in such circumstances as may be prescribed by the rules, to be treated as a party to any such proceedings and to be entitled to appear and to be heard accordingly.

(6) Rules of court relating to any such proceedings as are mentioned in subsection (5) of this section may provide for excluding so much of section 63(1) of the said Act of 1925 as requires appeals to the High Court to be heard and determined by a Divisional Court; but no appeal to the Court of Appeal shall be brought by virtue of this section except with the leave of the High Court or the Court of Appeal.

(7) In this section " decision" includes a direction, and references to the giving of a decision shall be construed accordingly.

(8) Without prejudice to section 4(5) of the 1961 Act, building regulations may in connection with any such appeal as is mentioned in subsection (1) above include such supplementary provisions with respect to procedure as the Secretary of State thinks fit.

70 Power to make building regulations for Inner London

(1) The following enactments (which relate to the power to make, and other matters connected with, building regulations), namely sections 61, 62 and 67 of the 1936 Act and sections 4(2) and (5) to (7), 5 and 9 of the 1961 Act, shall (with this Part, except section 75 and Schedule 7) apply throughout Inner London as they apply elsewhere in England and Wales; but without prejudice to that power as extended by this subsection, this subsection shall not of itself cause any building regulations made before it comes into force to apply to Inner London.

(2) Subject to any provision made by virtue of section 62(4), it shall be the duty of the Greater London Council to enforce in Inner London any building regulations which are in force there except to the extent that other local authorities or district surveyors within the meaning of the London Building Acts 1930 to 1939 are by virtue of building regulations made responsible for their enforcement there.

(3) Where by virtue of this section or section 62(4) local authorities or any prescribed person or class of persons (other than local authorities) are made responsible for enforcing, or performing prescribed functions under or in connection with, building regulations in force in Inner London, then, without prejudice to the said section 62(4), building regulations may in that connection provide for any prescribed provision falling within section 76(1)(a) or (b) but not mentioned in subsection (1) above to apply (with any prescribed modifications, and notwithstanding paragraph 12 or 34 of Part I of Schedule 11 to the London Government Act 1963) in relation to any such authority or person, or persons of any such class, as that provision applies in relation to a local authority outside Inner London.

(4) Without prejudice to the generality of section 62(5) building regulations may repeal or modify any provision to which this subsection applies if it appears to the Secretary of State that the repeal or, as the case may be, the modification of that provision is expedient in consequence of the provisions of this section or in connection with any provision contained in building regulations that apply to or to any part of Inner London.

(5) The preceding subsection applies to any provision—

(a) of the London Building Acts 1930 to 1939 ;

(b) of any enactment contained in this Act, other than this Part, or in any other Act passed before or in the same Session as this Act, in so far as that provision—

(i) applies to or to any part of Inner London ; and

(ii) relates to, or to the making of, byelaws for or for any part of Inner London with respect to any matter for or in connection with which provision can be made by building regulations ;

(c) of any byelaws made or having effect under the said Acts or of any such byelaws as are mentioned in paragraph (b)(ii) above.

(6) Before making any building regulations that provide for the repeal or modification of any provision to which the preceding subsection applies, the Secretary of State shall (without prejudice to the requirements as to consultation in section 9(3) of the 1961 Act) consult the Greater London Council and any other local authority who appear to him to be concerned.

(7) In this section " Inner London" means the area comprising the Inner London boroughs, the City, and the Inner Temple and the Middle Temple.

(8) In Part I of Schedule 11 to the London Government Act 1963 (modifications of Public Health Acts)—

(a) in paragraph 12, for the words " 53 to 55, and 57 to 71 " there shall be substituted the words " 54, 55, 57 to 60, 64 to 66, 69, 70 and (so far as unrepealed) 71 ";

(b) in paragraph 34, for the words " 4 to 11" there shall be substituted the words " 4(3) and (4), 6 to 8 and 10 and (except in so far as it amends any enactment mentioned in section 70(1) of the Health and Safety at Work etc. Act 1974) section 11 ".

71 Civil liability

(1) Subject to the provisions of this section, breach of a duty imposed by building regulations shall, so far as it causes damage, be actionable except in so far as the

regulations provide otherwise ; and as regards any such duty building regulations may provide for any prescribed defence to be available in any action for breach of that duty brought by virtue of this subsection.

(2) Subsection (1) above and any defence provided for in regulations made by virtue thereof shall not apply in the case of a breach of such a duty in connection with a building erected before the date on which that subsection comes into force unless the regulations imposing the duty apply to or in connection with the building by virtue of section 62 of the 1936 Act or section 65(2) of this Act.

(3) Nothing in this section shall be construed as affecting the extent (if any) to which breach—

(a) of a duty imposed by or arising in connection with this Part or any other enactment relating to building regulations; or

(b) of a duty imposed by building regulations in a case to which subsection (1) above does not apply,

is actionable, or as prejudicing any right of action which exists apart from the enactments relating to building regulations.

(4) In this section " damage " includes the death of, or injury to, any person (including any disease and any impairment of a person's physical or mental condition).

72 Application to Crown

(1) Except in so far as building regulations provide otherwise, the substantive provisions of building regulations—

(a) shall apply in relation to work carried out or proposed to be carried out by or on behalf of a Crown authority (whether or not in relation to a Crown building) as they would apply if the person by or on behalf of whom the work was or is to be carried out were not a Crown authority; and

(b) so far as they consist of continuing requirements, shall apply to Crown authorities (whether or not in relation to Crown buildings) as they apply to persons who are not Crown authorities.

(2) In so far as building regulations so provide as regards any of the substantive requirements of building regulations, those requirements shall apply in relation to work carried out or proposed to be carried out as mentioned in subsection (1)(a) above in Inner London and, so far as they consist of continuing requirements, shall apply to Crown authorities there as mentioned in subsection (1)(b) above, even if those requirements do not apply there in the case of work carried out or proposed to be carried out otherwise than by or on behalf of a Crown authority or, in the case of continuing requirements, do not apply there to persons other than Crown authorities.

In this subsection " Inner London " has the same meaning as in section 70.

(3) Except in so far as building regulations provide otherwise, building regulations and the enactments relating to building regulations—

(a) shall apply in relation to work carried out or proposed to be carried out in relation to a Crown building otherwise than by or on behalf of a Crown authority, and, in the case of section 65 and building regulations made by virtue thereof, shall in relation to a Crown building apply to persons other than Crown authorities, as they would apply if the building were not a Crown building; and

(b) shall apply in relation to work carried out or proposed to be carried out by or on behalf of a government department acting for a person other than a Crown authority as they would apply if the work had been or were to be carried out by that person.

(4) Section 341 of the 1936 Act (power to apply provisions of that Act to Crown property) shall not apply to provisions relating to building regulations.

(5) Section 71 and any building regulations made by virtue of subsection (1) of that section shall apply in relation to duties imposed by building regulations in their application in accordance with the preceding provisions of this section.

(6) In the case of work carried out or proposed to be carried out by or on behalf of a Crown authority, and in any case in which a Crown authority is or (apart from any dispensation or relaxation) will be subject to any continuing requirements, that authority may exercise the like powers of dispensing with or relaxing the substantive requirements of building regulations or, as the case may be, the continuing requirements in question as are conferred on the Secretary of State and local authorities by virtue of section 6 of the 1961 Act (other than a power excepted by the following subsection), subject, however, to the like requirements as to consultation (if any) as apply by virtue of section 62(1) in the case of a local authority (but not the requirements of the said section 6 as to consultation with the local authority) and to the like requirements as in the case of the Secretary of State apply by virtue of section 8 of that Act (opportunity to make representations about proposal to relax building regulations); and no application shall be necessary for the exercise of any such powers by virtue of this subsection.

In relation to any continuing requirements references in this subsection to the said section 6 are references thereto as modified by section 65(5).

(7) The power excepted from the preceding subsection is one which by virtue of section 62(4) is exercisable otherwise than by a local authority.

(8) For the purposes of subsection (6) above work carried out or proposed to be carried out by or on behalf of a government department acting for another Crown authority shall be treated as carried out or proposed to be carried out by or on behalf of that department (and not by or on behalf of the other Crown authority).

(9) In this section—

" continuing requirement " means a continuing requirement of building regulations imposed by virtue of section 65(1) or (2)(a) or (b).

" Crown authority " means the Crown Estate Commissioners, a Minister of the Crown, a government department, any other person or body whose functions are performed on behalf of the Crown (not being a person or body whose functions are performed on behalf of Her Majesty in her private capacity), or any person acting in right of the Duchy of Lancaster or the Duchy of Cornwall;

" Crown building " means a building in which there is a Crown interest or a Duchy interest;

" Crown interest " means an interest belonging to Her Majesty in right of the Crown or belonging to a government department, or held in trust for Her Majesty for the purposes of a government department;

" Duchy interest " means an interest belonging to Her Majesty in right of the Duchy of Lancaster, or belonging to the Duchy of Cornwall.

(10) If any question arises under this section as to which Crown authority is entitled to exercise any such powers as are mentioned in subsection (6) above, that question shall be referred to the Treasury, whose decision shall be final.

(11) The preceding provisions of this section shall, with any necessary modifications, apply in relation to the making of a material change in the use of a building within the meaning of building regulations made for the purposes of section 62(1)(e) of the 1936 Act (as substituted by this Part) as they apply in relation to the carrying out of work.

73 Application to United Kingdom Atomic Energy Authority

(1) The provisions of section 72, except subsections (2) to (4), shall apply in relation to the United Kingdom Atomic Energy Authority (in this section referred to as " the Authority ") as if—

- (a) the Authority were a Crown authority ;
- (b) any building belonging to or occupied by the Authority were a Crown building; and
- (c) the references in subsection (1) to not being a Crown authority were references to being neither a Crown authority nor the Authority,

but so that the said provisions shall not by virtue of this subsection apply in relation to dwelling-houses or offices belonging to or occupied by the Authority.

(2) Subject to the said provisions as applied by the preceding subsection, building regulations and the enactments relating to building regulations shall not apply in relation to buildings belonging to or occupied by the Authority, being buildings other than dwelling-houses or offices.

74 Meaning of " building" etc. in connection with, and construction of references to, building regulations

(1) For the purposes of any enactment to which this subsection applies—

- (a) " building " means any permanent or temporary building and, unless the context otherwise requires, includes any other structure or erection of whatever kind or nature (whether permanent or temporary), and in this paragraph, " structure or erection" shall include a vehicle, vessel, hovercraft, aircraft or other movable object of any kind in such circumstances as may be prescribed (being circumstances which in the opinion of the Secretary of State justify treating it for those purposes as a building);
- (b) unless the context otherwise requires, any reference to a building includes a reference to part of a building, and any reference to the provision of services, fittings and equipment in or in connection with buildings, or to services, fittings and equipment so provided, includes a reference to the affixing of things to buildings or, as the case may be, to things so affixed ; and
- (c) references to the construction or erection of a building shall include references to—
    - (i) the carrying out of such operations (whether for the reconstruction of a building, the roofing over of an open space between walls or buildings, or otherwise) as may be designated in building regulations as operations falling to be treated for those purposes as the construction or erection of a building, and

(ii) the conversion of a movable object into what is by virtue of paragraph (a) above a building,

and " construct" and " erect" shall be construed accordingly.

(2) The preceding subsection applies to sections 61 to 71 of the 1936 Act and to any other enactment (whether or not contained in the 1936 Act or this Act) which relates to building regulations or mentions " buildings " or " a building " in a context from which it appears that those expressions are there intended to have the same meaning as in the said sections 61 to 71.

(3) Unless the context otherwise requires, references in this Act or any other enactment (whether passed before or after this Act) to building regulations shall, in any particular case in relation to which any requirement of building regulations is for the time being dispensed with, waived, relaxed or modified by virtue of section 6 of the 1961 Act, section 66 of this Act or any other enactment, be construed as references to building regulations as they apply in that case.

75 Amendment of Building (Scotland) Act 1959

The Building (Scotland) Act 1959 shall have effect subject to the amendments provided for in Schedule 7.

76 Construction and interpretation of Part III and other provisions relating to building regulations

(1) The following provisions, namely—

(a) so much of Part II of the 1936 Act as relates to building regulations;

(b) so much of Part II of the 1961 Act as relates to building regulations; and

(c) this Part, except section 75 and Schedule 7 ;

shall be construed as one; and Part XII of the 1936 Act shall have effect as if the provisions mentioned in paragraph (b) and (c) above (as well as those mentioned in paragraph (a)) were contained in Part II of that Act.

(2) For the purposes of the provisions mentioned in subsection (1)(a) to (c) above—

(a) " local authority " means a district council, the Greater London Council, a London borough council, the Sub-Treasurer of the Inner Temple or the Under-Treasurer of the Middle Temple, and includes the Council of the Isles of Scilly; and

(b) the definitions of " local authority" in section 1 (2) of the 1936 Act and section 2(3) of the 1961 Act shall not apply;

and in section 1(1) of the 1961 Act (Part II of that Act to be construed as one with Part II of the 1936 Act), after the words " Part II of this Act" there shall be inserted the words " , except so much of it as relates to building regulations, ".

(3) In this Part—

" the 1936 Act " means the Public Health Act 1936;

" the 1961 Act " means the Public Health Act 1961 ;

" the substantive requirements of building regulations " means the requirements of building regulations with respect to the design and construction of buildings and the provision of services, fittings and equipment in or in connection with buildings (including requirements imposed by virtue of section 65(1) or (2)(a) or (b)), as distinct from procedural requirements.

(4) In this Part, in sections 61 to 71 of the 1936 Act and in sections 4 to 8 of the 1961 Act "prescribed" means prescribed by building regulations.

PART IV

MISCELLANEOUS AND GENERAL

77 Amendment of Radiological Protection Act 1970

(1) Section 1 of the Radiological Protection Act 1970 (establishment and functions of the National Radiological Protection Board) shall be amended in accordance with the following provisions of this subsection—

(a) after subsection (6) there shall be inserted as subsection (6A)—

"(6A) In carrying out such of their functions as relate to matters to which the functions of the Health and Safety Commission relate, the Board shall (without prejudice to subsection (7) below) act in consultation with the Commission and have regard to the Commission's policies with respect to such matters.";

(b) after subsection (7) there shall be inserted as subsections (7A) and (7B)—

"(7A) Without prejudice to subsection (6) or (7) above, it shall be the duty of the Board, if so directed by the Health Ministers, to enter into an agreement with the Health and Safety Commission for the Board to carry out on behalf of the Commission such of the Commission's functions relating to ionising or other radiations (including those which are not electro-magnetic) as may be determined by or in accordance with the direction; and the Board shall have power to carry out any agreement entered into in pursuance of a direction under this subsection.

(7B) The requirement as to consultation in subsection (7) above shall not apply to a direction under subsection (7A).";

(c) in subsection (8), after the words " subsection (7)" there shall be inserted the words " or (7A) ".

(2) In section 2(6) of the Radiological Protection Act 1970 (persons by whom, as regards premises occupied by the said Board, sections 1 to 51 of the Offices, Shops and Railway Premises Act 1963 and regulations thereunder are enforceable) for the words from " inspectors appointed " to the end of the subsection there shall be substituted the words " inspectors appointed by the Health and Safety Executive under section 19 of the Health and Safety at Work etc. Act 1974. "

78 Amendment of Fire Precautions Act 1971

(1) The Fire Precautions Act 1971 shall be amended in accordance with the following provisions of this section.

(2) In section 1(2) (power to designate uses of premises for which fire certificate is compulsory) at the end there shall be inserted as paragraph if)—

"(f) use as a place of work."

(3) In section 2 (premises exempt from section 1), paragraphs (a) to (c) (which exempt certain premises covered by the Offices, Shops and Railway Premises Act 1963, the Factories Act 1961 or the Mines and Quarries Act 1954) shall cease to have effect.

(4) After section 9 there shall be inserted as section 9A—

"9A Duty to provide certain premises with means of escape in case of fire.

(1) All premises to which this section applies shall be provided with such means of escape in case of fire for the persons employed to work therein as may reasonably be required in the circumstances of the case.

(2) The premises to which this section applies are—

(a) office premises, shop premises and railway premises to which the Offices, Shops and Railway Premises Act 1963 applies; and

(b) premises which are deemed to be such premises for the purposes of that Act,

being (in each case) premises in which persons are employed to work.

(3) In determining, for the purposes of this section, what means of escape may reasonably be required in the case of any premises, regard shall be had (amongst other things) not only to the number of persons who may be expected to be working in the premises at any time but also to the number of persons (other than those employed to work therein) who may reasonably be expected to be resorting to the premises at that time.

(4) In the event of a contravention of subsection (1) above the occupier of the premises shall be guilty of an offence and liable on summary conviction to a fine not exceeding £400."

(5) In section 12(1) (power to make regulations about fire precautions as regards certain premises), at the end there shall be added the words " and nothing in this section shall confer on the Secretary of State power to make provision with respect to the taking or observance of special precautions in connection with the carrying on of any manufacturing process.

(6) In section 17 (duty of fire authorities to consult other authorities before requiring alterations to buildings)—

(a) in subsection (1), the word " and" shall be omitted where last occurring in paragraph (i) and shall be added at the end of paragraph (ii), and after paragraph

(ii) there shall be added as paragraph (iii)—

"(iii) if the premises are used as a place of work and are within the field of responsibility of one or more enforcing authorities within the meaning of Part I of the Health and Safety at Work etc. Act 1974, consult that authority or each of those authorities.";

(b) in subsection (2) (clarification of references in section 9 to persons aggrieved), for the words " or buildings authority" there shall be substituted the words " buildings authority or other authority ";

(c) after subsection (2) there shall be added as subsection (3)—

"(3) Section 18(7) of the Health and Safety at Work etc. Act 1974 (meaning in Part I of that Act of ' enforcing authority' and of such an authority's ' field of responsibility ') shall apply for the purposes of this section as it applies for the purposes of that Part."

(7) In section 18 (enforcement of Act)—

(a) for the word " it" there shall be substituted the words " (1) Subject to subsection (2) below, it ";

(b) for the word "section" there shall be substituted the word " subsection "; and

(c) after the word " offence " there shall be added as subsection (2)—

"(2) A fire authority shall have power to arrange with the Health and Safety Commission for such of the authority's functions under this Act as may be specified in the arrangements to be performed on their behalf by the Health and Safety Executive (with or without payment) in relation to any particular premises so specified which are used as a place of work."

(8) In section 40 (application to Crown etc.)—

(a) in subsection (1)(a) (provisions which apply to premises occupied by the Crown), after the word " 6 " there shall be inserted the words " , 9A (except subsection (4)) ";

(b) in subsection (1)(b) (provisions which apply to premises owned, but not occupied by, the Crown), after the word " 8 " there shall be inserted the word " 9A ";

(c) in subsection (10) (application of Act to hospital premises in Scotland), for the words from " Regional " to " hospitals" there shall be substituted the words " Health Board ";

(d) after subsection (10) there shall be inserted the following subsection—

"(10A) This Act shall apply to premises in England occupied by a Board of Governors of a teaching hospital (being a body for the time being specified in an order under section 15(1) of the National Health Service Reorganisation Act 1973) as if they were premises occupied by the Crown.".

(9) In section 43(1) (interpretation) there shall be added at the end the following definition—

"" work " has the same meaning as it has for the purposes of Part I of the Health and Safety at Work etc. Act 1974".

(10) Schedule 8 (transitional provisions with respect to fire certificates under the Factories Act 1961 or the Offices, Shops and Railway Premises Act 1963) shall have effect.

79 Amendment of Companies Acts as to directors' reports

(1) The Companies Act 1967 shall be amended in accordance with the following provisions of this section.

(2) In section 16 (additional general matters to be dealt with in directors' reports) in subsection (1) there shall be added after paragraph (f)—

"(g) in the case of companies of such classes as may be prescribed by regulations made by the Secretary of State, contain such information as may be so prescribed about the arrangements in force in that year for securing the health, safety and welfare at work of employees of the company and its subsidiaries and for protecting other persons against risks to health or safety arising out of or in connection with the activities at work of those employees."

(3) After subsection (4) of the said section 16 there shall be added—

"(5) Regulations made under paragraph (g) of subsection (1) above may—

(a) make different provision in relation to companies of different classes;

(b) enable any requirements of the regulations to be dispensed with or modified in particular cases by any specified person or by any person authorised in that behalf by a specified authority ;

(c) contain such transitional provisions as the Secretary of State thinks necessary or expedient in connection with any provision made by the regulations.

(6) The power to make regulations under the said paragraph (g) shall be exercisable by statutory instrument which shall be subject to annulment in pursuance of a resolution of either House of Parliament.

(7) Any expression used in the said paragraph (g) and in Part I of the Health and Safety at Work etc. Act 1974 shall have the same meaning in that paragraph as it has in that Part of that Act and section 1(3) of that Act shall apply for interpreting that paragraph as it applies for interpreting that Part of that Act; and in subsection (5) above " specified" means specified in regulations made under that paragraph.".

80 General power to repeal or modify Acts and instruments

(1) Regulations made under this subsection may repeal or modify any provision to which this subsection applies if it appears to the authority making the regulations that the repeal or, as the case may be, the modification of that provision is expedient in consequence of or in connection with any provision made by or under Part I.

(2) Subsection (1) above applies to any provision, not being among the relevant statutory provisions, which—

(a) is contained in this Act or in any other Act passed before or in the same Session as this Act; or

(b) is contained in any regulations, order or other instrument of a legislative character which was made under an Act before the passing of this Act; or

(c) applies, excludes or for any other purpose refers to any of the relevant statutory provisions and is contained in any Act not falling within paragraph (a) above or in any regulations, order or other instrument of a legislative character which is made under an Act but does not fall within paragraph (b) above.

(3) Without prejudice to the generality of subsection (1) above, the modifications which may be made by regulations thereunder include modifications relating to the enforcement of provisions to which this section applies (including the appointment of persons for the purpose of such enforcement, and the powers of persons so appointed).

(4) The power to make regulations under subsection (1) above shall be exercisable—

(a) in relation to provisions not relating exclusively to agricultural operations, by the Secretary of State ;

(b) in relation to provisions relating exclusively to the relevant agricultural purposes, by the appropriate agriculture authority;

but before making regulations under that subsection the Secretary of State or the appropriate agriculture authority shall consult such bodies as appear to the Secretary of State or, as the case may be, that authority to be appropriate.

(5) Regulations under subsection (1) above in relation to provisions falling within subsection (4)(b) above may be either regulations applying to Great Britain and made by the Minister of Agriculture, Fisheries and Food and the Secretary of State acting jointly, or regulations applying to England and Wales only and made by the said Minister, or regulations applying to Scotland only and made by the Secretary of State; and in subsection (4)(b) above " the appropriate agriculture authority " shall be construed accordingly.

(6) In this section " the relevant statutory provisions," " the relevant agricultural purposes " and " agricultural operation " have the same meaning as in Part I.

81 Expenses and receipts

There shall be paid out of money provided by Parliament—

(a) any expenses incurred by a Minister of the Crown or government department for the purposes of this Act; and

(b) any increase attributable to the provisions of this Act in the sums payable under any other Act out of money so provided;

and any sums received by a Minister of the Crown or government department by virtue of this Act shall be paid into the Consolidated Fund.

82 General provisions as to interpretation and regulations

(1) In this Act—

(a) " Act" includes a provisional order confirmed by an Act;

(b) " contravention" includes failure to comply, and "contravene" has a corresponding meaning;

(c) " modifications" includes additions, omissions and amendments, and related expressions shall be construed accordingly;

(d) any reference to a Part, section or Schedule not otherwise identified is a reference to that Part or section of, or Schedule to, this Act.

(2) Except in so far as the context otherwise requires, any reference in this Act to an enactment is a reference to it as amended, and includes a reference to it as applied, by or under any other enactment, including this Act.

(3) Any power conferred by Part I or II or this Part to make regulations—

(a) includes power to make different provision by the regulations for different circumstances or cases and to include in the regulations such incidental, supplemental and transitional provisions as the authority making the regulations considers appropriate in connection with the regulations; and

(b) shall be exercisable by statutory instrument, which shall be subject to annulment in pursuance of a resolution of either House of Parliament.

83 Minor and consequential amendments, and repeals

(1) The enactments mentioned in Schedule 9 shall have effect subject to the amendments specified in that Schedule (being minor amendments or amendments consequential upon the provisions of this Act).

(2) The enactments mentioned in Schedule 10 are hereby repealed to the extent specified in the third column of that Schedule.

84 Extent, and application of Act

(1) This Act, except—

(a) Part I and this Part so far as may be necessary to enable regulations under section 15 or 30 to be made and operate for the purpose mentioned in paragraph 2 of Schedule 3 ; and

(b) paragraphs 2 and 3 of Schedule 9,

does not extend to Northern Ireland.

(2) Part III, except section 75 and Schedule 7, does not extend to Scotland.

(3) Her Majesty may by Order in Council provide that the provisions of Parts I and II and this Part shall, to such extent and for such purposes as may be specified in the Order, apply (with or without modification) to or in relation to persons, premises, work, articles, substances and other matters (of whatever kind) outside Great Britain as those provisions apply within Great Britain or within a part of Great Britain so specified. For the purposes of this subsection " premises", " work " and " substance " have the same meaning as they have for the purposes of Part I.

(4) An Order in Council under subsection (3) above—

(a) may make different provision for different circumstances or cases;

(b) may (notwithstanding that this may affect individuals or bodies corporate outside the United Kingdom) provide for any of the provisions mentioned in that subsection, as applied by such an Order, to apply to individuals whether or not they are British subjects and to bodies corporate whether or not they are incorporated under the law of any part of the United Kingdom;

(c) may make provision for conferring jurisdiction on any court or class of courts specified in the Order with respect to offences under Part I committed outside Great Britain or with respect to causes of action arising by virtue of section 47(2) in respect of acts or omissions taking place outside Great Britain, and for the determination, in accordance with the law in force in such part of Great Britain as may be specified in the Order, of questions arising out of such acts or omissions;

(d) may exclude from the operation of section 3 of the Territorial Waters Jurisdiction Act 1878 (consents required for prosecutions) proceedings for offences under any provision of Part I committed outside Great Britain;

(e) may be varied or revoked by a subsequent Order in Council under this section;

and any such Order shall be subject to annulment in pursuance of a resolution of either House of Parliament.

(5) In relation to proceedings for an offence under Part I committed outside Great Britain by virtue of an Order in Council under subsection (3) above, section 38 shall have effect as if the words " by an inspector, or " were omitted.

(6) Any jurisdiction conferred on any court under this section shall be without prejudice to any jurisdiction exercisable apart from this section by that or any other court.

85 Short title and commencement

(1) This Act may be cited as the Health and Safety at Work etc. Act 1974.

(2) This Act shall come into operation on such day as the Secretary of State may by order made by statutory instrument appoint, and different days may be appointed under this subsection for different purposes.

(3) An order under this section may contain such transitional provisions and savings as appear to the Secretary of State to be necessary or expedient in connection with the provisions thereby brought into force, including such adaptations of those provisions or any provision of this Act then in force as appear to him to be necessary or expedient in consequence of the partial operation of this Act (whether before or after the day appointed by the order).

SCHEDULES

SCHEDULE 1

Sections 1 and 53.

Existing Enactments which are Relevant Statutory Provisions

Chapter	Short Title	Provisions which are relevant statutory provisions
1875 c. 17.	The Explosives Act 1875.	The whole Act except sections 30 to 32, 80 and 116 to 121.
1882 c. 22.	The Boiler Explosions Act 1882.	The whole Act.
1890 c. 35.	The Boiler Explosions Act 1890.	The whole Act.
1906 c. 14.	The Alkali, &c. Works Regulation Act 1906.	The whole Act.
1909 c. 43.	The Revenue Act 1909.	Section 11.
1919 c. 23.	The Anthrax Prevention Act 1919.	The whole Act.
1920 c. 65.	The Employment of Women, Young Persons and Children Act 1920.	The whole Act.
1922 c. 35.	The Celluloid and Cinematograph Film Act 1922.	The whole Act.
1923 c. 17.	The Explosives Act 1923.	The whole Act.
1926 c. 43.	The Public Health (Smoke Abatement) Act 1926.	The whole Act.
1928 c. 32.	The Petroleum (Consolidation') Act 1928	The whole Act.
1936 c. 22.	The Hours of Employment (Conventions) Act 1936.	The whole Act except section 5.
1936 c. 27.	The Petroleum (Transfer of Licences) Act 1936	The whole Act.
1937 c. 45.	The Hydrogen Cyanide (Fumigation) Act 1937.	The whole Act.
1945 c. 19.	The Ministry of Fuel and Power Act 1945.	Section 1(1) so far as it relates to maintaining and improving the safety, health

Chapter	Short Title	Provisions which are relevant statutory provisions
		and welfare of persons employed in or about mines and quarries in Great Britain.
1946 c. 59.	The Coal Industry Nationalisation Act 1946.	Section 42(1) and (2).
1948 c. 37.	The Radioactive Substances Act 1948.	Section 5(1)(a).
1951 c. 21.	The Alkali, &c. Works Regulation (Scotland) Act 1951.	The whole Act.
1951 c. 58.	The Fireworks Act 1951.	Sections 4 and 7.
1952 c. 60.	The Agriculture (Poisonous Substances) Act 1952.	The whole Act.
1953 c. 47.	The Emergency Laws (Miscellaneous Provisions) Act 1953.	Section 3.
1954 c. 70.	The Mines and Quarries Act 1954.	The whole Act except section 151.
1956 c. 49.	The Agriculture (Safety, Health and Welfare Provisions) Act 1956.	The whole Act.
1961 c. 34.	The Factories Act 1961.	The whole Act except section 135.
1961 c. 64.	The Public Health Act 1961.	Section 73.
1962 c. 58.	The Pipe-lines Act 1962.	Sections 20 to 26,33,34 and 42, Schedule 5.
1963 c. 41.	The Offices, Shops and Railway Premises Act 1963.	The whole Act.
1965 c. 57.	The Nuclear Installations Act 1965.	Sections 1, 3 to 6, 22 and 24, Schedule 2.
1969 c. 10.	The Mines and Quarries (Tips) Act 1969.	Sections 1 to 10.
1971 c. 20.	The Mines Management Act 1971.	The whole Act.
1972 c. 28.	The Employment Medical Advisory Service Act 1972.	The whole Act except sections 1 and 6 and Schedule 1.

SCHEDULE 2

Section 10.

ADDITIONAL PROVISIONS RELATING TO CONSTITUTION ETC. OF THE COMMISSION AND EXECUTIVE

Tenure of office

1 Subject to paragraphs 2 to 4 below, a person shall hold and vacate office as a member or as chairman or deputy chairman in accordance with the terms of the instrument appointing him to that office.

2 A person may at any time resign his office as a member or as chairman or deputy chairman by giving the Secretary of State a notice in writing signed by that person and stating that he resigns that office.

3 (1) If a member becomes or ceases to be the chairman or deputy chairman, the Secretary of State may vary the terms of the instrument appointing him to be a member so as to alter the date on which he is to vacate office as a member.

(2) If the chairman or deputy chairman ceases to be a member he shall cease to be chairman or deputy chairman, as the case may be.

4 (1) If the Secretary of State is satisfied that a member—

(a) has been absent from meetings of the Commission for a period longer than six consecutive months without the permission of the Commission ; or

(b) has become bankrupt or made an arrangement with his creditors; or

(c) is incapacitated by physical or mental illness ; or

(d) is otherwise unable or unfit to discharge the functions of a member,

the Secretary of State may declare his office as a member to be vacant and shall notify the declaration in such manner as the Secretary of State thinks fit; and thereupon the office shall become vacant.

(2) In the application of the preceding sub-paragraph to Scotland for the references in paragraph (b) to a member's having become bankrupt and to a member's having made an arrangement with his creditors there shall be substituted respectively references to sequestration of a member's estate having been awarded and to a member's having made a trust deed for behoof of his creditors or a composition contract.

Remuneration etc. of members

5 The Commission may pay to each member such remuneration and allowances as the Secretary of State may determine.

6 The Commission may pay or make provision for paying, to or in respect of any member, such sums by way of pension, superannuation allowances and gratuities as the Secretary of State may determine.

7 Where a person ceases to be a member otherwise than on the expiry of his term of office and it appears to the Secretary of State that there are special circumstances which make it right for him to receive compensation, the Commission may make to him a payment of such amount as the Secretary of State may determine.

Proceedings

8 The quorum of the Commission and the arrangements relating to meetings of the Commission shall be such as the Commission may determine.

9 The validity of any proceedings of the Commission shall not be affected by any vacancy among the members or by any defect in the appointment of a member.

Staff

10 It shall be the duty of the Executive to provide for the Commission such officers and servants as are requisite for the proper discharge of the Commission's functions; and any reference in this Act to an officer or servant of the Commission is a reference to an officer or servant provided for the Commission in pursuance of this paragraph.

11 The Executive may appoint such officers and servants as it may determine with the consent of the Secretary of State as to numbers and terms and conditions of service.

12 The Commission shall pay to the Minister for the Civil Service, at such times in each accounting year as may be determined by that Minister subject to any directions of the Treasury, sums of such amounts as he may so determine for the purposes of this paragraph as being equivalent to the increase during that year of such liabilities of his as are attributable to the provision of pensions, allowances or gratuities to or in respect of persons who are or have been in the service of the Executive in so far as that increase results from the service of those persons during that accounting year and to the expense to be incurred in administering those pensions, allowances or gratuities.

Performance of functions

13 The Commission may authorise any member of the Commission or any officer or servant of the Commission or of the Executive to perform on behalf of the Commission such of the Commission's functions (including the function conferred on the Commission by this paragraph) as are specified in the authorisation.

Accounts and reports

14 (1) It shall be the duty of the Commission—

(a) to keep proper accounts and proper records in relation to the accounts;

(b) to prepare in respect of each accounting year a statement of accounts in such form as the Secretary of State may direct with the approval of the Treasury; and

(c) to send copies of the statement to the Secretary of State and the Comptroller and Auditor General before the end of the month of November next following the accounting year to which the statement relates.

(2) The Comptroller and Auditor General shall examine, certify and report on each statement received by him in pursuance of this Schedule and shall lay copies of each statement and of his report before each House of Parliament.

15 It shall be the duty of the Commission to make to the Secretary of State, as soon as possible after the end of each accounting year, a report on the performance of its functions during that year; and the Secretary of State shall lay before each House of Parliament a copy of each report made to him in pursuance of this paragraph.

Supplemental

16 The Secretary of State shall not make a determination or give his consent in pursuance of paragraph 5, 6, 7 or 11 of this Schedule except with the approval of the Minister for the Civil Service.

17 The fixing of the common seal of the Commission shall be authenticated by the signature of the secretary of the Commission or some other person authorised by the Commission to act for that purpose.

18 A document purporting to be duly executed under the seal of the Commission shall be received in evidence and shall, unless the contrary is proved, be deemed to be so executed.

19 In the preceding provisions of this Schedule—

(a) " accounting year " means the period of twelve months ending with 31st March in any year except that the first accounting year of the Commission shall, if the Secretary of State so directs, be such period shorter or longer than twelve months (but not longer than two years) as is specified in the direction ; and

(b) " the chairman ", " a deputy chairman " and " a member " mean respectively the chairman, a deputy chairman and a member of the Commission.

20 (1) The preceding provisions of this Schedule (except paragraphs 10 to 12 and 15) shall have effect in relation to the Executive as if—

(a) for any reference to the Commission there were substituted a reference to the Executive ;

(b) for any reference to the Secretary of State in paragraphs 2 to 4 and 19 and the first such reference in paragraph 7 there were substituted a reference to the Commission;

(c) for any reference to the Secretary of State in paragraphs 5 to 7 (except the first such reference in paragraph 7) there were substituted a reference to the Commission acting with the consent of the Secretary of State ;

(d) for any reference to the chairman there were substituted a reference to the director, and any reference to the deputy chairman were omitted;

(e) in paragraph 14(1)(c) for the words from "Secretary" to " following " there were substituted the words " Commission by such date as the Commission may direct after the end of ".

(2) It shall be the duty of the Commission to include in or send with the copies of the statement sent by it as required by paragraph 14(1)(c) of this Schedule copies of the statement sent to it by the Executive in pursuance of the said paragraph 14(1)(c) as adapted by the preceding sub-paragraph.

(3) The terms of an instrument appointing a person to be a member of the Executive shall be such as the Commission may determine with the approval of the Secretary of State and the Minister for the Civil Service.

SCHEDULE 3

Section 15.

SUBJECT-MATTER OF HEALTH AND SAFETY REGULATIONS

1 (1) Regulating or prohibiting—

(a) the manufacture, supply or use of any plant;
(b) the manufacture, supply, keeping or use of any substance;
(c) the carrying on of any process or the carrying out of any operation.

(2) Imposing requirements with respect to the design, construction, guarding, siting, installation, commissioning, examination, repair, maintenance, alteration, adjustment, dismantling, testing or inspection of any plant.

(3) Imposing requirements with respect to the marking of any plant or of any articles used or designed for use as components in any plant, and in that connection regulating or restricting the use of specified markings.

(4) Imposing requirements with respect to the testing, labelling or examination of any substance.

(5) Imposing requirements with respect to the carrying out of research in connection with any activity mentioned in sub-paragraphs (1) to (4) above.

2 (1) Prohibiting the importation into the United Kingdom or the landing or unloading there of articles or substances of any specified description, whether absolutely or unless conditions imposed by or under the regulations are complied with.

(2) Specifying, in a case where an act or omission in relation to such an importation, landing or unloading as is mentioned in the preceding sub-paragraph constitutes an offence under a provision of this Act and of the Customs and Excise Act 1952, the Act under which the offence is to be punished.

3 (1) Prohibiting or regulating the transport of articles or substances of any specified description.

(2) Imposing requirements with respect to the manner and means of transporting articles or substances of any specified description, including requirements with respect to the construction, testing and marking of containers and means of transport and the packaging and labelling of articles or substances in connection with their transport.

4 (1) Prohibiting the carrying on of any specified activity or the doing of any specified thing except under the authority and in accordance with the terms and conditions of a licence, or except with the consent or approval of a specified authority.

(2) Providing for the grant, renewal, variation, transfer and revocation of licences (including the variation and revocation of conditions attached to licences).

5 Requiring any person, premises or thing to be registered in any specified circumstances or as a condition of the carrying on of any specified activity or the doing of any specified thing.

6 (1) Requiring, in specified circumstances, the appointment (whether in a specified capacity or not) of persons (or persons with specified qualifications or experience, or both) to perform specified functions, and imposing duties or conferring powers on persons appointed (whether in pursuance of the regulations or not) to perform specified functions.

(2) Restricting the performance of specified functions to persons possessing specified qualifications or experience.

7 Regulating or prohibiting the employment in specified circumstances of all persons or any class of persons.

8 (1) Requiring the making of arrangements for securing the health of persons at work or other persons, including arrangements for medical examinations and health surveys.

(2) Requiring the making of arrangements for monitoring the atmospheric or other conditions in which persons work.

9 Imposing requirements with respect to any matter affecting the conditions in which persons work, including in particular such matters as the structural condition and stability of premises, the means of access to and egress from premises, cleanliness, temperature, fighting, ventilation, overcrowding, noise, vibrations, ionising and other radiations, dust and fumes.

10 Securing the provision of specified welfare facilities for persons at work, including in particular such things as an adequate water supply, sanitary conveniences, washing and bathing facilities, ambulance and first-aid arrangements, cloakroom accommodation, sitting facilities and refreshment facilities.

11 Imposing requirements with respect to the provision and use in specified circumstances of protective clothing or equipment, including clothing affording protection against the weather.

12 Requiring in specified circumstances the taking of specified precautions in connection with the risk of fire.

13 (1) Prohibiting or imposing requirements in connection with the emission into the atmosphere of any specified gas, smoke or dust or any other specified substance whatsoever.

(2) Prohibiting or imposing requirements in connection with the emission of noise, vibrations or any ionising or other radiations.

(3) Imposing requirements with respect to the monitoring of any such emission as is mentioned in the preceding sub-paragraphs.

14 Imposing requirements with respect to the instruction, training and supervision of persons at work.

15 (1) Requiring, in specified circumstances, specified matters to be notified in a specified manner to specified persons.

(2) Empowering inspectors in specified circumstances to require persons to submit written particulars of measures proposed to be taken to achieve compliance with any of the relevant statutory provisions.

16 Imposing requirements with respect to the keeping and preservation of records and other documents, including plans and maps.

17 Imposing requirements with respect to the management of animals.

18 The following purposes as regards premises of any specified description where persons work, namely—

(a) requiring precautions to be taken against dangers to which the premises or persons therein are or may be exposed by reason of conditions (including natural conditions) existing in the vicinity;

(b) securing that persons in the premises leave them in specified circumstances.

19 Conferring, in specified circumstances involving a risk of fire or explosion, power to search a person or any article which a person has with him for the purpose of ascertaining whether he has in his possession any article of a specified kind likely

in those circumstances to cause a fire or explosion, and power to seize and dispose of any article of that kind found on such a search.

20 Restricting, prohibiting or requiring the doing of any specified thing where any accident or other occurrence of a specified kind has occurred.

21 As regards cases of any specified class, being a class such that the variety in .the circumstances of particular cases within it calls for the making of special provision for particular cases, any of the following purposes, namely—

(a) conferring on employers or other persons power to make rules or give directions with respect to matters affecting health or safety ;

(b) requiring employers or other persons to make rules with respect to any such matters ;

(c) empowering specified persons to require employers or other persons either to make rules with respect to any such matters or to modify any such rules previously made by virtue of this paragraph ; and

(d) making admissible in evidence without further proof, in such circumstances and subject to such conditions as may be specified, documents which purport to be copies of rules or rules of any specified class made under this paragraph.

22 Conferring on any local or public authority power to make byelaws with respect to any specified matter, specifying the authority or person by whom any byelaws made in the exercise of that power need to be confirmed, and generally providing for the procedure to be followed in connection with the making of any such byelaws.

Interpretation

23 (1) In this Schedule " specified " means specified in health and safety regulations.

(2) It is hereby declared that the mention in this Schedule of a purpose that falls within any more general purpose mentioned therein is without prejudice to the generality of the more general purpose.

SCHEDULE 4

Section 32.

MODIFICATIONS OF PART I IN CONNECTION WITH AGRICULTURE

Provisions applied	*Modifications*
1. Section 13(1) (various powers).	(a) Paragraph (b) shall be omitted; (b) references to the Commission or the Secretary of State shall be read as references to the appropriate Agriculture Minister, so however that references to the Commission's functions shall be read as references to the functions of that Minister under the relevant statutory provisions in relation to matters relating exclusively to the relevant agricultural purposes.

Provisions applied	Modifications
2. Section 14 (power to direct investigations and inquiries).	(a) References to the Commission shall be read as references to the appropriate Agriculture Minister; (b) in subsection (1), the reference to the general purposes of Part I shall be read as a reference to the relevant agricultural purposes; (c) in subsection (2), for the words from " direct " to " other " in paragraph (a) there shall be substituted the words " authorise any ", the words " with the consent of the Secretary of State " shall be omitted, and for the words from " only matters " to the end of the subsection there shall be substituted the words " matters relating exclusively to the relevant agricultural purposes "; (d) in subsection (6), references to the Secretary of State shall be read as references to the appropriate Agriculture Minister.
3. Section 16 (approval of codes of practice).	(a) In subsection (1), the reference to health and safety regulations shall be read as a reference to agricultural health and safety regulations and the words from " and except " to " agricultural operations " shall be omitted, but so that the section shall confer power to approve or issue codes of practice for any provision mentioned in section 16(1) only for the purposes of the application of that provision to matters relating exclusively to the relevant agricultural purposes; (b) a code of practice may either be approved for Great Britain and be so approved by the Minister of Agriculture, Fisheries and Food and the Secretary of State acting jointly, or be approved for England and Wales only and be so approved by that Minister or be approved for Scotland only and be so approved by the Secretary of State, and the references to the Commission shall accordingly be read as references to the Agriculture Ministers or the said Minister or the Secretary of State as the case may require; (c) for subsection (2) there shall be substituted— "(2) Before approving a code of practice under subsection (1) above the Minister or Ministers proposing to

Provisions applied	*Modifications*
	do so shall consult the Commission and any other body that appears to him or them to be appropriate.”;
	(d)for subsection (5) there shall be substituted—
	“(5) The authority by whom a code of practice has been approved under this section may at any time withdraw approval from that code, but before doing so shall consult the same bodies as the authority would be required to consult under subsection (2) above if the authority were proposing to approve the code.”.
4. Section 17(3) (use of approved codes in criminal proceedings).	The reference to the Commission shall be read as a reference to the Agriculture Ministers or either of them.
5. Section 27 (obtaining of information).	(a) References to the Commission or the Executive shall be read as references to the appropriate Agriculture Minister, so however that references to the Commission's functions shall be read as references to the functions of that Minister under the relevant statutory provisions in relation to matters relating exclusively to the relevant agricultural purposes;
	(b) references to an enforcing authority's functions shall be read as references to an enforcing authority's functions under the relevant statutory provisions in relation to matters relating exclusively to the relevant agricultural purposes;
	(c) in subsection (1), the words " with the consent of the Secretary of State " shall be omitted;
	(d) in subsection (2)(b), the reference to the Secretary of State shall be read as a reference to the appropriate Agriculture Minister, and the words " and the recipient of the information " shall be omitted.

SCHEDULE 5

Section 61.

SUBJECT-MATTER OF BUILDING REGULATIONS

1 Preparation of sites.

2 Suitability, durability and use of materials and components (including surface finishes).

3 Structural strength and stability, including—

(a) precautions against overloading, impact and explosion ;

(b) measures to safeguard adjacent buildings and services ;

(c) underpinning.

4 Fire precautions, including—

(a) structural measures to resist the outbreak and spread of fire and to mitigate its effects ;

(b) services, fittings and equipment designed to mitigate the effects of fire or to facilitate fire-fighting ;

(c) means of escape in case of fire and means for securing that such means of escape can be safely and effectively used at all material times.

5 Resistance to moisture and decay.

6 Measures affecting the transmission of heat

7 Measures affecting the transmission of sound.

8 Measures to prevent infestation.

9 Measures affecting the emission of smoke, gases, fumes, grit or dust or other noxious or offensive substances.

10 Drainage (including waste disposal units).

11 Cesspools and other means for the reception, treatment or disposal of foul matter.

12 Storage, treatment and removal of waste.

13 Installations utilising solid fuel, oil, gas, electricity or any other fuel or power (including appliances, storage tanks, heat exchangers, ducts, fans and other equipment).

14 Water services (including wells and bore-holes for the supply of water) and fittings and fixed equipment associated therewith.

15 Telecommunications services (including telephones and radio and television wiring installations).

16 Lifts, escalators, hoists, conveyors and moving footways.

17 Plant providing air under pressure.

18 Standards of heating, artificial lighting, mechanical ventilation and air-conditioning and provision of power outlets.

19 Open space about buildings and the natural lighting and ventilation of buildings.

20 Accommodation for specific purposes in or in connection with buildings, and the dimensions of rooms and other spaces within buildings.

21 Means of access to and egress from buildings and parts of buildings.

22 Prevention of danger and obstruction to persons in and about buildings (including passers-by).

23 Matters connected with or ancillary to any of the matters mentioned in the preceding provisions of this Schedule.

SCHEDULE 6

Section 61.

AMENDMENTS OF ENACTMENTS RELATING TO BUILDING REGULATIONS

PART I

AMENDMENTS

Amendments of Public Health Act 1936

1 In section 64 of the 1936 Act (passing or rejection of plans)—

(a) for subsection (3) substitute—

> "(3) Where plans of any proposed work deposited with a local authority are rejected in pursuance of the preceding provisions of this section, the person by whom or on whose behalf they were deposited may appeal against the rejection to the Secretary of State within the prescribed time and in the prescribed manner; and where the rejection results wholly or partly from the fact that a person or body whose approval or satisfaction in any respect is required by the regulations has withheld approval or not been satisfied, an appeal under this subsection may be brought on (or on grounds which include) the ground that the person or body in question ought in the circumstances to have approved or been satisfied in that respect."; and

(b) subsection (4) shall cease to have effect.

2 In section 65 of the 1936 Act (power to require removal or alteration of work not in conformity with building regulations etc.)—

(a) in subsection (1), after "therein" insert " and additions thereto and to execute such additional work in connection therewith ";

(b) after subsection (2) insert as subsection (2A)—

> "(2A) Where a local authority have power to serve a notice under subsection (1) or (2) above on the owner of any work, they may in addition or instead serve such a notice on one or more of the following persons, namely the occupier and any builder or other person appearing to the authority to have control over the work.";

(c) in subsection (3), after " therein " insert " and additions thereto and execute such additional work in connection therewith " , and at the end add as a proviso—

> "Provided that where a notice under subsection (1) or (2) above is given to two or more persons in pursuance of subsection (2A) above, then—

(a) if they are given the notices on different dates, the said period of twenty-eight days shall for each of them run from the later or latest of those dates; and

(b) if the notice is not complied with before the expiration of the said period or such longer period as a court of summary jurisdiction may on the application of any of them allow, any expenses recoverable as aforesaid may be recovered from any of them."; and

(d) in subsection (4), for " or subsection (2)" substitute " , (2) or (2A) " , and at the end add as a proviso—

"Provided that, in a case where plans were deposited nothing in this subsection shall be taken to prevent such a notice from being given (before the expiration of twelve months from the completion of the work in question) in respect of anything of which particulars were not required to be shown in the plans.".

3 In section 90 of the 1936 Act (interpretation of Part II of that Act)—

(a) in subsection (2) (extended meaning, in that Part and building regulations, of references to the erection of a building), for the words from " and, so far " to " those regulations " substitute " except sections 61 to 71 and any other enactment to which section 74(1) of the Health and Safety at Work etc. Act 1974 applies "; and

(b) for subsection (3) (meaning of references to deposited plans) substitute—

"(3) In this Part of this Act, unless the context otherwise requires.—

(a) any reference to the deposit of plans in accordance with building regulations shall be construed as a reference to the deposit of plans in accordance with those regulations for the purposes of section 64 of this Act; and

(b) " plans" includes drawings of any other description and also specifications or other information in any form, and any reference to the deposit of plans shall be construed accordingly."

Amendments of Public Health Act 1961

4 In section 4 of the 1961 Act (power to make building regulations)—

(a) in subsection (2) (power to make different provision for different areas) at the end add " and generally different provision for different circumstances or cases "; and

(b) in subsection (6) (penalties for contravening building regulations) after " building regulations" insert " other than a provision designated in the regulations as one to which this subsection does not apply, ", and for " one hundred pounds " and " ten pounds " substitute respectively " £400 " and "£50".

5 In section 6 of the 1961 Act (power to dispense with or relax requirements of building regulations)—

(a) in subsection (1), add at the end the words " either unconditionally or subject to compliance with any conditions specified in the direction, being conditions with respect to matters directly connected with the dispensation or relaxation. ";

(b) in the proviso to subsection (2), for the words from " shall " onwards substitute " may except applications of any description ";
(c) for subsection (6) substitute—

"(6) An application by a local authority in connection with a building or proposed building in the area of that authority shall be made to the Secretary of State except where the power of giving the direction is exercisable by that authority.";

(d) after subsection (7), there shall be inserted as subsections (7A) and (7B)—

"(7A) If, on an application to the Secretary of State for a direction under this section, the Secretary of State considers that any requirement of building regulations to which the application relates is not applicable or is not or would not be contravened in the case of the work or proposed work to which the application relates, he may so determine and may give any directions that he considers necessary in the circumstances.

(7B) A person who contravenes any condition specified in a direction given under this section or permits any such condition to be contravened shall be liable to a fine not exceeding £400 and to a further fine not exceeding £50 for each day on which the offence continues after he is convicted. and";

(e) subsection (8) shall be omitted.

6 In section 7 of the 1961 Act (appeal against local authority's refusal to dispense with or relax requirements of building regulations)—
(a) in subsection (1), after second " relax " insert " or grant such an application subject to conditions ", for " by notice in writing " substitute " in the prescribed manner ", for " one month" substitute " the prescribed period " and for " refusal" substitute " decision on the application ";
(b) in subsection (2), for the words from " a period " to " and the local authority " substitute " the prescribed period ";
(c) subsections (3) to (6) shall be omitted ; and
(d) at the end there shall be added the following subsection:—

"(7) Section 6(7A) of this Act shall apply in relation to an appeal to the Secretary of State under this section as it applies in relation to an application to him for a direction under section 6.".

7 For section 8 of the 1961 Act (advertisement of proposal to relax building regulations) substitute—

"8 Opportunity to make representations about proposal to relax building regulations.

"8 "8 Opportunity to make representations about proposal to relax building regulations.

(1) Before the Secretary of State or a local authority give a direction under section 6 of this Act the prescribed steps shall be taken for affording to persons likely to be affected by the direction an opportunity to make representations about it; and before giving the direction the Secretary of State

or, as the case may be, the local authority shall consider any representations duly made in accordance with the regulations.

(2) Building regulations—

(a) may make provision as to the time to be allowed for making representations under the preceding subsection ;

(b) may require an applicant for such a direction, as a condition that his application shall be entertained, to pay or undertake to pay the cost of publishing any notice which is required by the regulations to be published in connection with the application; and

(c) may exclude the requirements of the preceding subsection in prescribed cases.".

8 In section 9(3) of the 1961 Act (consultation with Building Regulations Advisory Committee and other bodies before making building regulations), at the end add " (including in particular, as regards regulations relevant to any of their functions, the National Water Council). ".

PART II

Public Health Act 1936 Section 65 and Public Health Act 1961 Sections 4, 6 and 7 as amended

"The Public Health Act 1936

65 (1) If any work to which building regulations are applicable contravenes any of those regulations, the authority, without prejudice to their right to take proceedings for a fine in respect of the contravention, may by notice require the owner either to pull down or remove the work or, if he so elects, to effect such alterations therein and additions thereto and to execute such additional work in connection therewith as may be necessary to make it comply with the regulations.

(2) If, in a case where the local authority are by any section of this Act other than the last preceding section expressly required or authorised to reject plans, any work to which building regulations are applicable is executed either without plans having been deposited, or notwithstanding the rejection of the plans, or otherwise than in accordance with any requirements subject to which the authority passed the plans, the authority may by notice to the owner either require him to pull down or remove the work, or require him either to pull down or remove the work or, if he so elects, to comply with any other requirements specified in the notice, being requirements which they might have made under the section in question as a condition of passing plans.

(2A) Where a local authority have power to serve a notice under subsection (1) or (2) above on the owner of any work, they may in addition or instead serve such a notice on one or more of the following persons, namely the occupier and any builder or other person appearing to the authority to have control over the work.

(3) If a person to whom a notice has been given under the foregoing provisions of this section fails to comply with the notice before the expiration of twenty-eight days, or such longer period as a court of summary jurisdiction may on his application allow, the local authority may pull down or remove the work in question, or effect such alterations therein and additions thereto and execute such additional work in connection therewith

as they deem necessary, and may recover from him the expenses reasonably incurred by them in so doing:

Provided that where a notice under subsection (1) or (2) above is given to two or more persons in pursuance of subsection (2A) above, then—

(a) if they are given the notices on different dates, the said period of twenty-eight days shall for each of them run from the later or latest of those dates ; and

(b) if the notice is not complied with before the expiration of the said period or such longer period as a court of summary jurisdiction may on the application of any of them allow, any expenses recoverable as aforesaid may be recovered from any of them.

(4) No such notice as is mentioned in subsection (1), (2) or (2A) of this section shall be given after the expiration of twelve months from the date of the completion of the work in question, and, in any case where plans were deposited, it shall not be open to the authority to give such a notice on the ground that the work contravenes any building regulation or, as the case may be, does not comply with their requirements under any such section of this Act as aforesaid, if either the plans were passed by the authority, or notice of their rejection was not given within the prescribed period from the deposit thereof, and if the work has been executed in accordance with the plans and of any requirement made by the local authority as a condition of passing the plans:

Provided that, in a case where plans were deposited, nothing in this subsection shall be taken to prevent such a notice from being given (before the expiration of twelve months from the completion of the work in question) in respect of anything of which particulars were not required to be shown in the plans.

(5) Nothing in this section shall affect the right of a local authority, or of the Attorney-General, or any other person, to apply for an injunction for the removal or alteration of any work on the ground that it contravenes any regulation or any enactment in this Act, but if the work is one in respect of which plans were deposited and the plans were passed by the local authority, or notice of their rejection was not given within the prescribed period after the deposit thereof, and if the work has been executed in accordance with the plans, the court on granting an injunction shall have power to order the local authority to pay to the owner of the work such compensation as the court thinks just, but before making any such order the court shall in accordance with rules of court cause the local authority, if not a party to the proceedings, to be joined as a party thereto.

The Public Health Act 1961

4 (1) . . . .

(2) Any provision contained in building regulations may be made so as to apply generally, or in an area specified in the regulations, and the regulations may make different provision for different areas and generally different provision for different circumstances or cases.

(3) It shall be the function of every local authority to enforce building regulations in their district.

(4) Local authorities shall, in relation to building regulations, have all such functions under sections 64 and 65 of the Public Health Act 1936 (which confer power to pass plans, and to enforce building byelaws) as they have in relation to building byelaws.

(5) Building regulations may include such supplemental and incidental provisions as appear to the Secretary of State to be expedient.

(6) If a person contravenes or fails to comply with any provision contained in building regulations, other than a provision designated in the regulations as one to which this subsection does not apply, he shall be liable to a fine not exceeding £400 and to a further fine not exceeding £50 for each day on which the default continues after he is convicted.

(7) The power of making building regulations shall be exercisable by statutory instrument which shall be subject to annulment in pursuance of a resolution of either House of Parliament.

6 (1) Subject to the provisions of this section, if the Secretary of State, on an application made in accordance with the provisions of this Act, considers that the operation of any requirement in building regulations would be unreasonable in relation to the particular case to which the application relates, he may after consultation with the local authority, give a direction dispensing with or relaxing that requirement either unconditionally or subject to compliance with any conditions specified in the direction, being conditions with respect to matters directly connected with the dispensation or relaxation.

(2) If building regulations so provide as regards any requirement contained in the regulations, the power to dispense with or relax that requirement under subsection (1) of this section shall be exercisable by the local authority (instead of by the Secretary of State after consultation with the local authority):

Provided that any building regulations made by virtue of this subsection may except applications of any description.

(3) Building regulations may provide as regards any requirement contained in the regulations that the foregoing subsections of this section shall not apply.

(4) An application under this section shall be in such form ....and shall contain such particulars as may be................................. prescribed.

(5) The application shall be made to the local authority and, except where the power of giving the direction is exercisable by the local authority, the local authority shall at once transmit the application to the Secretary of State and give notice to the applicant that it has been so transmitted.

(6) An application by a local authority in connection with a building or proposed building in the area of that authority shall be made to the Secretary of State except where the power of giving the direction is exercisable by that authority.

(7) The provisions of Part I of the First Schedule to this Act shall have effect as regards any application made under this section for a direction which will affect the application of building regulations to work which has been carried out before the making of the application.

(7A) If, on an application to the Secretary of State for a direction under this section, the Secretary of State considers that any requirement of building regulations to which the application relates is not applicable or is not or would not be contravened in the case of the work or proposed work to which the application relates he may so determine and may give any directions that he considers necessary in the circumstances.

(7B) A person who contravenes any condition specified in a direction given under this section or permits any such condition to be contravened shall be liable to a fine not exceeding

£400 and to a further fine not exceeding £50 for each day on which the offence continues after he is convicted.

7 (1) If a local authority refuse an application to dispense with or relax any requirement in building regulations which they have power to dispense with or relax, or grant such an applicatiion subject to conditions, the applicant may in the prescribed manner appeal to the Secretary of State within the prescribed period from the date on which the local authority notify the applicant of their decision on the application.

(2) If within the prescribed period the local authority do not notify the applicant of their decision on the application, subsection (1) of this section shall appply in relation to the application as if the local authority had refused the application and notified the applicant of their decision at the end of the said period.

. . . .

(7) Section 6(7A) of this Act shall apply in relation to an appeal to the Secretary of State under this section as it applies in relation to an application to him for a direction under section 6."

SCHEDULE 7

Section 75.

AMENDMENTS OF BUILDING (SCOTLAND) ACT 1959

1 In section 3 (building standards regulations)—

(a) in subsection (2), after the words "health, safety" there shall be inserted the word " welfare ", and at the end there shall be added the words " and for furthering the conservation of fuel and power ";

(b) in subsection (3), there shall be added the words—

"(d) be framed to any extent by reference to a document published by or on behalf of the Secretary of State or any other person.";

(c) at the end of the section there shall be added the following subsection—

"(7) The Secretary of State may by order made by statutory instrument repeal or modify any enactment to which this subsection applies if it appears to him that the enactment is inconsistent with, or is unnecessary or requires alteration in consequence of, any provision contained in the building standards regulations.

This subsection applies to any enactment contained in any Act passed before or in the same Session as the Health and Safety at Work etc. Act 1974 other than an enactment contained in the Building (Scotland) Act 1959."

2 In section 4 (relaxation of building standards regulations)—

(a) for subsection (5) there shall be substituted the following subsections—

"(5) A direction under subsection (1)(b) above—

(a) shall, if it so provides, cease to have effect at the end of such period as may be specified in the direction ;

(b) may be varied or revoked by a subsequent direction of the Secretary of State.

(5A) If at any time a direction under subsection (1)(b) above ceases to have effect by virtue of subsection (5)(a) above or is varied or revoked under subsection (5)(b) above, that fact shall not affect the continued operation of the direction (with any conditions specified therein) in any case in which before that time an application for a warrant in connection with the construction or change of use of a building, part or all of which is of the class to which the direction relates, was, in accordance with regulations made under section 2 of this Act, lodged with a buildings authority.";

(b) in subsections (6) and (7), after the words " subsection (1)(b)" there shall be inserted the words " or (5)(&) ";

(c) after subsection (7) there shall be inserted the following subsection :—

"(7A) A person making an application under subsection (1)(b) above shall pay to the Secretary of State such fee as may be prescribed ; and regulations made by virtue of this subsection may prescribe different fees for different cases:

Provided that the Secretary of State may in any particular case remit the whole or part of any fee payable by virtue of this subsection.".

3 After section 4A, there shall be inserted the following section—

"4B Power of Secretary of State to approve types of building, etc.

"4B "4B Power of Secretary of State to approve types of building, etc.

(1) The following provisions of this section shall have effect with a view to enabling the Secretary of State, either on an application made to him in that behalf or of his own accord, to approve any particular type of building as conforming, either generally or in any class of case, to particular provisions of the building standards regulations.

(2) An application for the approval under this section of a type of building shall be made in the prescribed manner.

(3) Where under subsection (1) above the Secretary of State approves a type of building as conforming to particular provisions of the building standards regulations either generally or in any class of case, he may issue a certificate to that effect specifying—

(a) the type of building to which the certificate relates;

(b) the provisions of the building standards regulations to which the certificate relates ; and

(c) where applicable, the class or classes of case to which the certificate applies.

(4) A certificate under this section shall, if it so provides, cease to have effect at the end of such period as may be specified in the certificate.

(5) If, while a certificate under this section is in force, it is found, in any particular case involving a building of the type to which the certificate relates, that the building in question is of that type and the case is one to which the certificate applies, that building shall in that particular case be

deemed to conform to the provisions of the building standards regulations to which the certificate relates.

(6) The Secretary of State may from time to time vary a certificate under this section either on an application made to him in that behalf or of his own accord ; but in the case of a certificate issued on an application made by a person under subsection (1) above, the Secretary of State, except where he varies it on the application of that person, shall before varying it give that person reasonable notice that he proposes to do so.

(7) A person making an application under subsection (1) or (6) above shall pay to the Secretary of State such fee as may be prescribed ; and regulations made by virtue of this subsection may prescribe different fees for different cases:

Provided that the Secretary of State may in any particular case remit the whole or part of any fee payable by virtue of this subsection.

(8) The Secretary of State may at any time revoke a certificate issued under this section, but before doing so shall give the person, if any, on whose application the certificate was issued reasonable notice that he proposes to do so.

(9) Where the Secretary of State issues a certificate under this section or varies or revokes a certificate so issued, he shall publish notice of that fact in such manner as he thinks fit.

(10) If at any time a certificate under this section ceases to have effect by virtue of subsection (4) above or is varied or revoked under the preceding provisions of this section, that fact shall not affect the continued operation of subsection (5) above by virtue of that certificate in any case in which before that time an application for a warrant in connection with the construction of a type of building to which the certificate relates was, in accordance with regulations made under section 2 of this Act, lodged with a buildings authority.

(11) For the purposes of subsection (3) above or any variation of a certificate under subsection (6) above, a class of case may be framed in any way that the Secretary of State thinks fit."

4 In section 6 (application of building standards regulations and building operations regulations to construction or demolition, and to change of use, of buildings)—

(a) after subsection (3) there shall be inserted the following subsection—

"(3A) Notwithstanding that a buildings authority are not satisfied that the information submitted to them with an application for a warrant for the construction of a building is sufficient in respect of such stage in the construction as may be prescribed to show that the building when constructed will not fail to conform to the building standards regulations, they may grant a warrant for the construction of the building but subject to the condition that work on such prescribed stage shall not be proceeded with until such further information relating to that stage as they may require is submitted to them and until they have made an amendment to the terms of the warrant authorising such work to proceed:

Provided that they shall, subject to subsection (8) of this section, make such an amendment on application being made therefor in the prescribed manner only if they are satisfied that nothing in the information submitted to them in respect of the prescribed stage shows that that stage when constructed will fail to conform to the building standards regulations.";

(b) in subsection (10), after the words " any such " there shall be inserted the words " prescribed stage as is mentioned in subsection (3A) of this section and any such ".

5 In section 9 (certificates of completion)—

(a) in subsection (2), for the words " but only if, they are satisfied that" there shall be substituted the words " , so far as they are able to ascertain after taking all reasonable steps in that behalf, ";

(b) in subsection (3), for the words, " be satisfied as mentioned in the last foregoing subsection " there shall be substituted the words " grant a certificate of completion ";

(c) after subsection (3) there shall be inserted the following subsection—

"(3A) In respect of so much of a building as consists of such an installation as may be prescribed, not being an electrical installation, a buildings authority shall not grant a certificate of completion unless there is produced to them a certificate granted by a person of such class as may be prescribed certifying that the installation complies with such of the said conditions as relate to it:

Provided that this subsection shall not apply in a case where it is shown to the satisfaction of the buildings authority that for some reasonable cause such a certificate cannot be produced.";

(d) in subsection (4) for the words " the last foregoing subsection " there shall be substituted the words " subsection (3) or (3A) above ".

6 In section 11(1)(b) (power of local authorities to require buildings to conform to building standards regulations), after the words " health, safety " there shall be inserted the word " welfare ", and after the word " generally " there shall be inserted the words " and for furthering the conservation of fuel and power ".

7 In section 19 (penalties), for the words " ten pounds " and " one hundred pounds ", wherever they occur, there shall be substituted respectively the words " £50 " and " £400 ".

8 After section 19 there shall be inserted the following section—

"19A Civil liability

"19A "19A Civil liability

(1) Subject to the provisions of this section, a breach to which this section applies shall, so far as it causes damage, be actionable except in so far as may be otherwise prescribed ; and in any action brought by virtue of this subsection such defence as may be prescribed shall be available.

(2) This section applies to the following breaches—

(a) failure to comply with the terms or conditions of a warrant for the construction, demolition or change of use of a building or with any order under this Act relating to the construction of a building;

(b) contravention of any provision of the building operations regulations ;

(c) constructing a building without a warrant otherwise than in accordance with the building standards regulations ;

(d) changing the use of a building without a warrant where after the change of use the building does not conform to so much of the building standards regulations as become applicable, or apply more onerously, to the building by reason of the change of use.

(3) Subsection (1) above and any defence provided for in regulations made by virtue thereof shall not apply in the case of a breach to which this section applies in connection with a building erected before the date on which that subsection comes into force unless the breach arises in relation to the change of use, extension, alteration, demolition, repair, maintenance or fitting of such a building.

(4) Nothing in this section shall be construed as affecting the extent (if any) to which a breach to which this section applies is actionable in a case to which subsection (1) above does not apply, or as prejudicing any right of action which exists apart from the provisions of this section.

(5) In this section " damage" includes the death of, or injury to, any person (including any disease and any impairment of a person's physical or mental condition)."

9 In section 26 (Crown rights)—

(a) in subsection (1) after the words " Crown and " there shall be inserted the words " subject to the provisions of this section ";

(b) after subsection (2) there shall be inserted the following subsections—

"(2A) The building standards regulations shall, except in so far as they otherwise prescribe, apply to a Crown building as they would apply if the building were not a Crown building.

(2B) A Crown building to which the building standards regulations apply shall be constructed in accordance with those regulations.

(2C) Any extension to or alteration of a Crown building to which the building standards regulations apply or would apply on the extension or alteration of the building shall not cause the building as extended or altered, as a direct result of the extension or, as the case may be, the alteration—

(a) if it conformed to the building standards regulations immediately before the date of commencement of the operations, to fail to conform to them ; or

(b) if it failed to conform to the building standards regulations immediately before that date, to fail to conform to them to a greater degree than that to which it failed to conform immediately before that date ;

and any change of use of a Crown building shall not cause the building after the change of use to fail to conform to so much of the building standards regulations as will become applicable, or will apply more onerously, to the building by reason of the change of use.

(2D) Section 19A of this Act shall apply to a Crown building as it applies to a building other than a Crown building, but as if for subsection (2) there were substituted the following subsection:—

"(2) A breach to which this section applies is a failure to comply with subsection (2B) or (2C) of section 26 of this Act or a contravention of any provision of the building operations regulations".

(2E) Without prejudice to any case to which proviso (a) to subsection (1) above is applicable, the Secretary of State shall have the like powers of dispensing with or relaxing the provisions of the building standards regulations in relation to a Crown building as he has under section 4(1) of this Act in relation to a building other than a Crown building ; and subsections (3), (4), (5), (5A) and (9) of the said section 4 shall apply for the purposes of this section as if—

(a) in subsection (4), the words " or, as the case maybe, the buildings authority " were omitted ;

(b) in subsection (5A), for the words from " an application " to the end there were substituted the words " the construction or change of use of a building, part or all of which is of the class to which the direction relates, was begun ";

(c) in subsection (9), the words "or section 4A(3) of this Act" were omitted.

(2F) Without prejudice to any case to which the said proviso is applicable, in the application of section 4B of this Act to a Crown building, subsection (10) shall have effect as if for the words from " an application " to the end there were substituted the words " the construction of a building, part or all of which is of the type to which the certificate relates, was begun.".

SCHEDULE 8

Section 78.

Transitional Provisions with respect to Fire Certificates under Factories Act 1961 or Offices, Shops and Railway Premises Act 1963

1 In this Schedule—

" the 1971 Act " means the Fire Precautions Act 1971 ;

" 1971 Act certificate" means a fire certificate within the meaning of the 1971 Act;

" Factories Act certificate " means a certificate under section 40 of the Factories Act 1961 (means of escape in case of fire-certification by fire authority);

" Offices Act certificate" means a fire certificate under section 29 of the Offices, Shops and Railway Premises Act 1963.

2 (1) Where by virtue of an order under section 1 of the 1971 Act a 1971 Act certificate becomes required in respect of any premises at a time when there is in force in respect of those premises a Factories Act certificate or an Offices Act certificate (" the existing certificate"), the following provisions of this paragraph shall apply.

(2) The existing certificate shall continue in force (irrespective of whether the section under which it was issued remains in force) and—

(a) shall as from the said time be deemed to be a 1971 Act certificate validly issued with respect to the premises with respect to which it was issued and to cover the use or uses to which those premises were being put at that time; and

(b) may (in particular) be amended, replaced or revoked in accordance with the 1971 Act accordingly.

(3) Without prejudice to sub-paragraph (2)(b) above, the existing certificate, as it has effect by virtue of sub-paragraph (2) above, shall as from the said time be treated as imposing in relation to the premises the like requirements as were previously imposed in relation thereto by the following provisions, that is to say—

(a) if the existing certificate is a Factories Act certificate, the following provisions of the Factories Act 1961, namely sections 41(1), 48 (except subsections (5), (8) and (9)), 49(1), 51(1) and 52(1) and (4) and, so far as it relates to a proposed increase in the number of persons employed in any premises, section 41(3);

(b) if the existing certificate is an Offices Act certificate the following provisions of the Offices, Shops and Railway Premises Act 1963, namely sections 30(1), 33, 34(1) and (2), 36(1) and 38(1) and, so far as it relates to a proposed increase in the number of persons employed to work in any premises at any one time, section 30(3).

3 Any application for a Factories Act certificate or an Offices Act certificate with respect to any premises which is pending at the time when by virtue of an order under section 1 of the 1971 Act a 1971 Act certificate becomes required in respect of those premises shall be deemed to be an application for a 1971 Act certificate in respect of them duly made in accordance with the 1971 Act and may be proceeded with accordingly; but (without prejudice to section 5(2) of the 1971 Act) the fire authority may, as a condition of proceeding with such an application, require the applicant to specify any matter or give them any information which would ordinarily have been required by section 5(1) of that Act.

SCHEDULE 9

Section 83.

Minor and Consequential Amendments

The Coroners (Amendment) Act 1926

1 In section 13(2)(c) of the Coroners (Amendment) Act 1926 (by virtue of which an inquest must be held with a jury in cases of death from certain causes of which notice is required to be given to any inspector or other officer of a government department), after the words "of a government department" there shall be inserted the words " or to an inspector appointed under section 19 of the Health and Safety at Work etc. Act 1974 ".

The House of Commons Disqualification Act 1957

2 In Part II of Schedule 1 to the House of Commons Disqualification Act 1957 (which specifies bodies of which all members are disqualified under that Act), as it applies to the House of Commons of the Parliament of the United Kingdom, there shall be inserted at the appropriate place in alphabetical order the words " The Health and Safety Commission ".

The Parliamentary Commissioner Act 1967

3 In Schedule 2 to the Parliamentary Commissioner Act 1967 (which lists the authorities subject to investigation under that Act) there shall be inserted in the appropriate places in alphabetical order the words " Health and Safety Commission " and " Health and Safety Executive ".

SCHEDULE 10

Section 83.

REPEALS

Chapter	Short Title	Extent of Repeal
26 Geo. 5 & 1 Edw. 8. c. 49.	The Public Health Act 1936.	Section 53.
		Section 64(4) and (5).
		In section 67, the words from " and the Secretary of State's decision " to the end of the section.
		Section 71.
		In section 343(1), the definition of " building regulations ".
7 & 8 Geo. 6. c. 31.	The Education Act 1944.	Section 63(1).
10 & 11 Geo. 6. c. 51.	The Town and Country Planning Act 1947.	In Schedule 8, the amendment of section 53 of the Public Health Act 1936.
2 & 3 Eliz. 2. c. 32.	The Atomic Energy Authority Act 1954.	Section 5(5).
4 & 5 Eliz. 2. c. 52.	The Clean Air Act 1956.	Section 24.
9 & 10 Eliz. 2. c. 64.	The Public Health Act 1961.	In section 4, subsection (1) and, in subsection (4), the words from " and building " to the end of the subsection.
		In section 6, in subection (4), the words " as may be prescribed by building

Chapter	Short Title	Extent of Repeal
		regulations " and the word " so ", and subsection (8).
		Section 7(3) to (6).
		Section 10(1) and (2).
		In Schedule 1, in Part III, the amendments of sections 53,61, 62 and 71 of the Public Health Act 1936 and, in the amendments of the Clean Air Act 1956, the amendment of section 24 and the word " twenty-four" in the last paragraph.
1965 c. 16.	The Airports Authority Act 1965.	In section 19(3), the words from " and section 71 " to " regulations) " and the words " and the proviso to the said section 71 ".
1971 c. 40.	The Fire Precautions Act 1971.	In section 2, paragraphs (a) to (c).
		Section 11.
		In section 17(1)(i), the word " and " where last occurring.
		In section 43(1), the definition of " building regulations ".
1971 c. 75.	The Civil Aviation Act 1971.	In Schedule 5, in paragraph 2(1), the words from " and section 71 " to " regulations)" and the words " and the proviso to the said section 71 ".
1972 c. 28.	The Employment Medical Advisory Service Act 1972.	Sections 1 and 6.
		Schedule 1.
1972 c. 58.	The National Health Service (Scotland) Act 1972.	In Schedule 6, paragraph 157.
1972 c. 70.	The Local Government Act 1972.	In Schedule 14, paragraph 43.
1973 c. 32.	The National Health Service Reorganisation Act 1973.	In Schedule 4, paragraph 137.
1973 c. 50.	The Employment and Training Act 1973.	In Schedule 3, paragraph 14.

Chapter	Short Title	Extent of Repeal
1973 c. 64.	The Maplin Development Act 1973.	In Schedule 2, in paragraph 2(1), the words from " and section 71" to " regulations) ".

Adapted and published by GRANGIS under the OGL Licence 3.0.

www.nationalarchives.gov.uk/doc/open-government-licence/version/3/

GRANGIS - UK PUBLISHING 2022.

Thank you for taking the time to leave us a review regarding this version

★★★★★

For further inquiries, contact us at:
www.grangis.com / contact@grangis.com

www.ingramcontent.com/pod-product-compliance
Lightning Source LLC
LaVergne TN
LVHW060213210926
848481LV00008B/2722
9798885590976